What others are saying about
*How To Live With Your Partner And Enjoy it**

This small book contains a vast amount of wisdom and insight that will be helpful to all couples and individuals who wish to enhanve their lives in relationship.

ERVING POLSTER, PH.D., AUTHOR AND CLINICAL PSYCHOLOGIST

In my nearly 40 years if conducting marriage and couples counseling, I wished I had a small comprehensive book for couples. I did not have one—but now, with Don Hanley's new release, present and future counselors have such a book, and one that will be a valuable guide for couples for years to come.

JOSEPH D. DILLON, PH.D., LMFT, RETIRED PROFESSOR AND COUNSELOR

This is the first book that successfully covers most of the important issues that couples bring in marriage counseling. It is a very positive approach to problem solving in relationships. I highly recommend it to couples who are serious about enriching their relationships.

DEBORAH SHRIVER, M.A., LMFT AND DIRECTOR OF COUNSELING AT NORTH SAN DIEGO COUNTY LIFELINE COMMUNITY SERVICES

How to Live with Your Partner and Enjoy it was previously published as *Visiting Angels & Home Devils*, also published by A Word with You Press in 2010. It has been updated and revised.

Also by Don Hanley:

How to Live with Yourself and Enjoy it

"How to Live With Yourself and Enjoy it is a true treasure. Using an easy, conversational tone, and sharing stories from his own fascinating, yet highly relatable life, Dr. Don Hanley succeeds in creating a book that is deeply engaging, highly accessible, and—to use his own term—profoundly 'life-giving.'"

GHADA OSMAN, PH.D. ,UNIVERSITY OF HARVARD GRADUATE, PRACTICING LMFT

How to Live with
YOUR PARTNER
and *Enjoy it*

A Discussion Guide for Couples

*... on enhancing the strength and love
and diminishing the faults
in each of us*

Don Hanley, MFT, Ph.D.

TOP READS PUBLISHING, LLC

Vista, California

How to Live with Your Partner and Enjoy it
is published by:

Top Reads Publishing, LLC

For information, please direct emails to:
info@topreadspublishing.com or visit our website:
www.topreadspublishing.com

Cover design and interior layout: Teri Rider

First Edition, July 2016

Originally published under the title, *Visiting Angels & Home Devils*, also published by A Word with You Press in 2010. It has been revised and updated.

Printed in the United States of America

10 9 8 7 6 5 4 3 2   25

DEDICATION

I want to dedicate this book to the hundreds of interns and clients I have worked with over the years. Thank all of you for sharing your stories with me and opening your hearts to me.

Don Hanley

FOREWORD

This is a revised edition of an earlier book entitled *Visiting Angels and Home Devils*. I have changed the title in order to be companionable with *How to Live with Yourself and Enjoy it*, and *How to Live with Your Children and Enjoy it*, and create a three-volume set the reader will find useful for various stages of their life.

I hope you have read *How to Live with Yourself and Enjoy it*. If you have, you will notice some of the same themes in this book. If not, I have made this book complete in itself. I have rewritten part of the text, adding more personal comments to make the reading more informal. I delighted in the illustrations created by Niehl Zulueta for the first edition, so I will reprint them here—the depictions of people with wings or with horns still express two of our many sides.

The old title of *Visiting Angels and Home Devils* is still a valid one for most marriages, as many of us are more cordial and likable to those outside the family than we are to those within. Many years ago, my daughter Micaela, now forty-one, and I had a disagreement and she was quite angry with me. I said, "Well, my students and clients like me." She responded, "Yeah, but they don't have to live with you!" Our families are our truth tellers, teachers, and our balancers that we need, if we really want to grow as persons.

This small book will not attempt to tell you, step-by-step, how to have a happy marriage or partnership. If I did, you wouldn't follow it anyway—we are all too wonderfully unique and independent. Each couple has the delightful challenge of creating their own "perfect" union. I will simply bring up some important ideas that I have found to be helpful to the many couples I have worked with in couples therapy—and challenges I am still working on in my personal life. I am in my eighties and have been married forty-six years. I have also worked as a psychotherapist and marriage counselor for over forty of those years. I have seen many changes not only in myself but in our society. I am still learning—and my wife, Anne, agrees that I have a lot more to learn.

The reason I am using the title *How to Live with Your Partner and Enjoy it* and use "Partner" and not "Spouse," is that there are an increasing number of people who live together but are not married, and there are gay and lesbian couples, some who are married and some who are not. Married or not, we live together because we care about one another, and most often, if it is not merely for economic reasons (to share the rent), it is because we love one another. I will sometimes use the words "marriage," "spouse," or "husband and wife," but the ideas are applicable to all intimate relationships, married or not.

Before I was a teenager, I learned and sang love songs. I still like the sentiment and many of the ideals, like love makes men Kings and women Queens and that we'll stay in love forever. Even in my youth, I knew the lyrics rarely brought up the struggles and problems couples encounter on the road to "true" love. It is a road well worth traveling and I hope you will find my words helpful.

Don Hanley

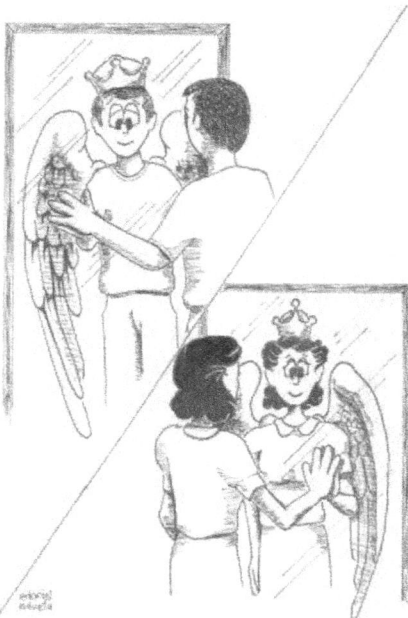

TABLE OF CONTENTS

Chapter 1

ON BEING NATURAL BORN LOVERS –
IT IS STILL NOT EASY

It is up to us to give our relationships a chance.
There is nothing greater in life than loving another and
being loved in return, for loving is the ultimate of experiences

Leo Buscaglia

BORN TO LOVE AND THE CHALLENGE
OF LEARNING HOW

In 1970, I married a wonderful, beautiful, intelligent, and loving woman. Had I known then what I know now, we both would have had a more pleasant journey. I had been a Catholic priest and had many years of college and had taught and counseled many people about relationships, love, and marriage. A few years ago, I found a box full of my old papers and a copy of a talk I had given to a group of teachers about love. It was an articulate and understandable speech about something of which I really had very little experience: love, and especially romantic love. They seemed to be only abstract ideas to me at the time. I hope that this and later chapters will be more helpful than that speech was.

I still have many convictions and opinions about lots of things. Right now, two convictions stand out: Every living person is far more gifted, more lovable, and stronger than they were taught to believe, and their challenge in life is to develop that strength and those gifts and become even more lovable. We are born to be in loving connection with other human beings, and true love begins with seeing ourselves and other persons as being worth and deserving of respect, no matter who we are and who they are. Simply attempting to follow the example of our parents or some other *ideal* couple is never sufficient.

Einstein eloquently said, "No problem can be solved with the same consciousness that caused the problem in the first place." And this applies to our human development as well as all other life challenges. For many centuries humans have had to spend all waking hours foraging for food and shelter. It was a physical survival consciousness. Now our consciousness, at least in the developed world, is able to rise above our ancestors' all-consuming search for food and shelter. Now, we can devote a great deal of our time and energy enhancing our emotional, intellectual, and spiritual lives. This is part of our "new" consciousness.

When physical survival was the primary goal, finding a strong and healthy mate was a survival goal also. A man looked for a strong female who could bear healthy children. A woman looked for a strong male who could be a successful hunter and protector of the family. Many anthropologists believe that we have continued to inherit this same trait. Modern life has affected it so that now, an average man looks for a healthy and beautiful mate, and the woman still looks for a strong successful mate—not to hunt but for financial security.

ON BEING STRONG, GIFTED, AND FINDING OUR TRUE SELVES

In order to have a truly loving marriage or any kind of healthy partnership, it is important that we have a positive and healthy sense of self—an honest acceptance of who we are. Our psychological and spiritual health begins when we are in our mother's womb. If our mothers were physically and emotionally healthy, did not smoke or take unhealthy drugs, and were treated lovingly by their partner, then we began life in a very positive way. If we were nurtured and loved in our early years, we thrived, and arrived at adulthood able to be a supportive and loving mate to someone. Unfortunately, too few people begin life in this utopian way.

My own beginning in 1933, the worst year of the Great Depression, was far from being utopian. Before my mother became pregnant with me, she had twelve previous pregnancies—eight live births and four miscarriages. One infant brother and one eight-year-old sister died two years before I was born, so my mother was seriously depressed. She did not want another child and abortion was not considered, even if it had been available. So into this world I came. My dad was also depressed because he had lost his farm due to the Depression and a start-up trucking business had failed. I was an adult before I realized they were heroic in just surviving and finding basic necessities for their children.

Through no fault of my own, nor fault of my parents, I began life with an uncertain future. I did have many challenges and made good and bad decisions while I coped with finding my gifts and strengths as I bumbled along into adulthood. Many spiritual writers indicate that we all have a *true* self within us that is connected to the divine or to the universe of the wonderful unconscious, and that we must find it by first experiencing a *false* self on our road to discovering and living that true self.

I prefer to call our journey as the development of our *exploratory* self. Calling it a false self sounds too negative and indicates that it is our fault that we *have* a false self. My belief is that it is just part of our natural evolution—something that we must go through and, hopefully, experience as a challenge and even as an adventure on our journey as we become more authentic and true. I like to think that our true self is the "stardust" that Carl Sagan and now Neal Tyson say we humans are made of. Our challenge is to become aware of our wonderful self. When we love ourselves, we can more fully love another. Too many of us never learn to love ourselves.

If we are fortunate and have worked to be aware of our choices, and have taken responsibility for our decisions, we will arrive at adulthood and be ready for marriage. We will have some sense of who we are and what we wish to make of our lives. Again, consciousness comes into the picture: Do I want to make lots of money and achieve great power in business and industry? Or do I only want to look beautiful as a woman, or muscular and buff as a man, so I look successful or stand out in my corner of society? Do I want to make a contribution and help the world become a better place by promoting life, education, health, safety, peace, and love? Or could it be, I just don't care what happens to those around me; I just want to enjoy life in any way I can? Perhaps, I want to have a bit of all the above.

I do not believe it is realistic or even healthy to expect ourselves, or others, to have some kind of set accomplishments before we can think of getting married. Hopefully, we just have some realistic goals and ideas of how to reach them and we would like to have a partner who would be willing to share the journey with us. As I write this, I realize that when I was young, I often heard that by the age of twenty-five, a person should know what they wanted to do the rest of their lives, where they were going to live, and with whom they wanted to spend their lives. Stability was seen as a primary virtue. I believe that, because of our parents' and grandparents' hard work and stability, we now can see that our personal, relational, and spiritual growth can be seen as an adventure that can, and will, enhance our lives and the lives of others. So hope and a sense of adventure have replaced stability as primary virtues. I fantasize that you will hope with me.

My beliefs about life's journey began in the first grade, and were light-years away from thinking I was wonderful in any way. I had already received so many negative messages that I believed I probably was the dumbest, clumsiest, ugliest, and must unlovable kid on the planet. Most of the messages came from my six older brothers and sisters. I was scared nearly to death as I walked through the classroom door on the first day of school. I wet my pants and was sent home before the morning recess so often, I flunked the first grade. That verified all the negatives that I thought defined me.

That didn't begin to change until I was eleven years old and I began to shine in school and as a worker. One positive thing I learned from those earlier experiences was that I should be kind to people—especially little kids. When I was eleven, my parents divorced and I made the decision to stay with my dad and work with him at the lumberyard. Having the choice of with whom and where to live was the greatest gift of my young life.

At age twelve, I made another momentous decision—I would become a priest so I could help people be kind and loving. Dad died when I was fourteen and I closed down emotionally and became a very sad young fellow. I avoided being completely depressed by working hard every waking hour. I bought a house when I was eighteen for my mom and two youngest sisters. When I was 21, I built a rental house on the property so Mom would have some income when I left for the seminary.

I did become a priest and managed to grow into a fairly gentle person by the time I decided to get married at age thirty-seven. Right before our wedding, I sold the houses and paid for our wedding and, later, for my doctoral studies. Of course, I didn't plan on that but it was a nice outcome of my "Gloomy Gus" (as two or three of my siblings called me) workaholic years.

After I began feeling the wonderful glow of romantic love, I thought that I probably was a phony during my years as a priest. Six years after our marriage and after moving to California, and having two beautiful daughters and obtaining a Ph.D. in psychology, we took our first trip back to Kansas. I looked up the priest's housekeeper I had gotten to know quite well when I was in Wichita, Kansas. She was a delightful elderly African-American woman who had asked me to read and write letters to and from her grown children. She had retired and had bought a small home in a good neighborhood. She delighted in Anne and both of our daughters. She gave me the most wonderful compliment I have ever received: "You know, Father— Oh, I know you're not a Father anymore, but you're still Father to me. Anyhow,

I was a priest's housekeeper for over thirty-five years, and you were different from all the other priests I ever saw." I asked her how I was different and she said, "Well, I knew in your heart, you thought I was just as good as the bishops, the old monsignor, the rich white folks, and everybody else." I was stunned. I felt so good, it almost erased those bad feelings I had kept with me since I was a young child. Note: I said, "almost."

Now, at age eighty-three, I can look back and realize I had learned a lot about life and love, and how to live with mistakes and failures and successes. Everyone develops a "script", narrative or story, about who they are and how they should live to survive and grow. We discover our unconscious script by reflecting on our thoughts, feelings, and reactions to people and events in our lives. In my case, you can guess that my script would be quite confusing and have some strong positives as well as negatives. I had a great deal of fear of others—especially people in any kind of authority; I must work hard to survive; I am ugly and stupid and people do not like me. People might not like me, but might like what I do if I work hard and am studious. The script I developed commanded that I work alone so I would be able to avoid criticism and condemnation.

I must do good to others if I am to become a worthy person. I thought that my six married siblings were unhappy in their marriage, so I believed that I would find happiness elsewhere—I would become a priest. I put that in my script when I was twelve. Of course, none of this was clear when I was a child or adolescent; it became clear after years of reflection.

Take a look at your own journey and no matter how *good* or *bad* it was, see it as an adventure you managed to survive. After all these years I can look back and see how all this helped me to understand others. How has your journey helped you? As a therapist I have often asked clients if they could give themselves a pat on the back just for surviving all they had been through. My story had some challenges and sad experiences, but I learned, as a priest and therapist, many people I have had the privilege to know had even greater challenges.

On Being Born To Be In Loving Connection With Others

I wanted to continue working with people and so, after leaving the priesthood, I became a psychologist and marriage and family therapist. As I mentioned, I have worked in that profession for over forty years. In all those years, I have never worked with a depressed person who was not also isolated from other people. Many felt isolated, not because they didn't have people around, but because they had never learned to let others *in*. They may have many reasons. The most common is a deep seated belief that they are not worthy of love because of what they had been told by parents, teachers, and/or religious ministers. They think, *If you knew me like I really am, you could not love me*. Their scripts included a very negative core belief that they were *bad* in some intrinsic way. I have lost count of the many clients who said, "I know there is something wrong with me." Almost always, there is nothing *wrong* with them, other than perhaps having made some bad choices along the way and not realizing that no one is perfect. We humans are creations and not perfect beings.

That no one is perfect was brought home to me one time when I was a priest and hearing confessions before a Saturday morning mass. A young voice said through the screen, "Bwess me Fado, for I have sinned. My last confession was one day ago, and this is my second confession."

I interrupted her and said, "My child, why are you in here again if you just went to confession yesterday?"

She responded, "Well, Fado, nobody is purrfeck."

I don't know what her *new* sin was because I was working too hard to keep from laughing.

We feel inadequate and *bad* because we still have some growing to do. Unfortunately, few people tell us that; they just point out all the things we do wrong, and what is *bad* about us.

I believe that we are naturally good, or as *Star Wars* puts it: The Force is with us. We can ignore it but this Amazing Grace is still there. We do not need to *earn* it; our challenge is just to let it blossom forth. Personal change is like the rosebud becoming a fully blossomed rose— it does not become a tulip. Everyone is worthy of love. Is the Dali Lama more worthy of love than a new born baby, or a mischievous seven year old?

Many people I have worked with believe that they must be *perfect* if they are ever able to be loved and be happy. One of the absolute truths I hold onto is that no one is perfect, nor will anyone be able to become perfect—because we are limited, finite, and breakable beings. Your husband or your wife, or your best friend, or you, are not perfect, and will not become perfect either. I do have a strong prejudice against those persons who act like they are perfect. The key word here is ACT. Too many religions teach that we must be perfect if we want to continue belonging to that church, or get to heaven. What they mean by *being perfect* is that members must follow all the rules of that particular religion. If it is a Christian religion, that sect has forgotten Jesus' words: "The law was made for man, not man for the law." Legalism is not perfection; it is only a source of a psychological dictum called obsessive-compulsive disorder—OCD. It also prevents a person from loving and being loved in a life-giving way.

So, allow your imperfect self to get to know other imperfect selves. If you continue on a path of care and awareness, you will find someone who is just the right person to share your life with in a special intimate way and begin living together and growing together—learning how to live with your partner and enjoy it. The greatest gift we can give another is our own gentle and caring self.

ON RESPECTING ANOTHER PERSON NO MATTER WHO THEY ARE AND WHO WE ARE

A strong and gentle person sees other people in a life-giving way; that is, we let them know we appreciate what they do with and for us and others and that we like having their presence in our lives. Dr. Martin Buber, a philosophy professor in the early twentieth century, developed a theory of human relationships that has influenced a great deal of modern-day therapy. He tells this story that profoundly influenced him: As a young professor, he counseled an anxious and depressed student. After an hour of listening and gently advising the young man, the fellow left. Three hours later, another student ran into Buber's office and exclaimed that the young man had hung himself. He was dead. For hours and days, Buber pondered the session with the boy. He believed that he had been a decent counselor—he had listened, did not over-advise, was compassionate. So, what went wrong? After many days of thought, he realized that one big error he made was this: He left the boy in the role of student and counselee, and he, Buber, remained in the role of professor and counselor. It was a role-to-role encounter, not a person-to-person exchange. Buber called the person-to-person encounter an *I-Thou* connection. The I-Thou relationship is life-giving, whereas the role-to-role or *I-IT* relationship can be, but often is not.

Unfortunately, I have worked with many couples who were living in an I-It relationship. They were husband and wife, not Bob and Susan. So, one of the challenges of couples counseling is to coach them into seeing one another in the deepest possible way—to allow themselves to resonate with the other's anguish, sadness, disappointment, joy, feelings of elation and accomplishment. There is no "right way" to do this, only a sincere connecting way. I encourage both partners to be able to sit with their own pain as well as their partner's without trying to hide it, fake it, or fix it. Of course, this is true for counselors as well.

One of the main reasons I left the priesthood was that I was expected to be in a role by the majority of people I met and worked with. I often heard people say, "You don't talk like a priest." Or "You don't act like a priest." Usually this was meant as a compliment, but too often as a scolding. Some men get used to it and are authentically themselves. I found it difficult to simply be myself. It was a lonely journey for me that became dehumanizing, especially if I tried to be conforming and work to impose rigid moral dictates such as the prohibition of *artificial* birth control.

Going back to the first conviction: After working with hundreds of people in individual and couples therapy and teaching hundreds more in college and graduate school, I have learned and re-learned that every one of us is far more loving than we believe and act. And one of the most important learning grounds for us to become more loving and stronger is in our intimate partnerships and marriage.

WHEN TO HUG AND WHEN TO RUN

We will often encounter people who have some characteristics and habits that will attract us and some will disturb us. These people we may just casually meet and others we may become partners with, in dating situations, serious coupling, living together, and/or "going all the way and getting married." Please take a look at each item below and the end words—*Run* or *Hug*. As you think of your partner and yourself, evaluate him or her and yourself as huggable or not on the list of possible traits. Your partner may be someone you are dating, engaged to, or now "hitched to." If you are not married, you might want to ditch the partner if his or her *Run* items far outnumber your *Hug* items—especially if he or she is not willing to discuss and possibly change. If you see yourself as having too many *Run* items, you may want to slow down the dating game, or engagement, and work on your own growth. Put a big *IF* after each Run item because if the person has this kind of fault but is sincerely willing to work on it, then there is hope.

Of course, this would be true for you as well. In order not to keep saying he or she, or him or her, I will alternate the genders with each pair of sayings. I will not keep repeating "you and your partner"—just assume you are to look at yourself.

- If you and your partner have a cool head and a warm heart – Hug.
- If you and your partner have a hot head and a cold heart – Run or Fix.
- If your partner is open to your ideas, is interested in what you are doing but not trying to be part of everything you do – Hug.
- If your partner thinks she already knows what is best about everything you think, feel, and do – Run.
- If your partner is open to new ideas and your ideas about many things – Hug.
- If your partner is constantly nagging you about the way to do and say everything – Run.
- If your partner easily forgives you for seemingly everything you do – Hug.
- If your partner keeps reminding you of past mistakes or 'sins' – Run.
- If your partner thinks that sex and intimacy are the same thing – Run.
- If your partner believes that sex is the expression of your intimacy – Hug.
- If your partner says, "I love you, Baby," and then treats you like one – Run.
- If your partner cherishes you and delights in your efforts – Hug.
- If your partner tries to control your every move, feeling, and thought – Run.

- If your partner treats her mother and father with respect and warmth – Hug.
- If your partner, three consecutive times, lets his mother interrupt your intimate moments together – Run.
- If your partner is comfortable with his body and enjoys affection – Hug.
- If your partner is nervous about his body and wants you to always take the initiative – Run.
- If your partner notices other men, and unselfconsciously shares her thoughts – Hug.
- If your partner is constantly comparing you with other women in a negative way – Run.
- If your partner asks only "Did you have a good time?" when you've been away – Hug.
- If your partner always wants to know exactly where you were, who you were with, and what you did – Run.
- If your partner feels sadness and anguish when he hears of spousal or child abuse – Hug.
- If your partner regularly gets angry and hurts you physically as well as emotionally – Run fast.
- If your partner drinks too much alcohol or takes too many illegal drugs and doesn't think it is a 'big deal' and won't consider working on it – Run fast.

Of course, I could go on and on but I'm sure you get the idea. If you have married someone who seems to have too many of the *Run* items, then, if he or she is not endangering you emotionally or physically, patiently let him or her know how you feel when he or she acts or talks in hurtful ways. Too often we wait until we are fed up to *here* (usually the nose), then lash out angrily or tearfully and push our partner away. Often we or our partners don't realize that they or we are being hurtful—we are just acting and talking like everyone else did in the family we grew up with and it is "Just the way I am."

We will continue to explore these ideas so you and your partner will fit this illustration

(Without wings, of course.):

DISCUSSION POINTS

- *WRITE out a few ideas you have about being more positive toward yourself and your partner.*

- *ONE STUDY found that, before marriage, couples share five appreciations for every negative complaint, but this is reversed after marriage. How are you and your partner doing on this?*

- *WHAT are some changes you have made in yourself since you began your current relationship?*

- *Are they more positive or negative? If negative, will you change them?*

- *DO YOU initiate positive change in your relationship or wait until after your partner changes?*

Chapter 2

ON LEARNING TO BE LOVING PARTNERS

*Every word, facial expression, gesture, or action on the part
of a parent gives the child some message about self-worth. It
is sad that so many parents don't realize what message they
are sending.*

Virginia Satir, Pioneer in Family Therapy

ON DEVELOPING OUR ABILITY TO LOVE

Take a moment and look at the list of "Hugs and Run" items in the last
chapter. Think of how your mom and dad would rate on these items
when you were growing up. If one of them had to *run* from the other
a great deal of the time, you too, as a child and adolescent, paid a price.
At the very least you had a poor example from which to learn.

In my book *How to Live with Yourself and Enjoy It*, I wrote about
being a loving person, and included this paragraph: *When I speak of
love, I mean a power that is stronger than fear. I mean a kind of energy that
breathes meaning into life. It is an energy that defies nature's tendency to
diminish and destroy life, but causes us to grow and flourish in every way.
It is the triumph of the human spirit that allows us to overcome the distances
between us brought on by our selfish tendencies. True love even triumphs
over death.*

This is, of course, an ideal that we may feel we reach only a
few times in our lives, but it is not only the love that the poets and
songwriters are thinking of. I know that I thought of love that way,
and was motivated by that reality, when I fell in love with Anne. And I

still do. If we are to become a loving person, we must first learn how to accept and love ourselves. If we do not love ourselves, the love will be tainted by pity—and deep down we resent pity. Don't be like Groucho Marx who said, "I would never belong to a club that would have me as a member."

A colleague with whom I was discussing being a loving person, said, "Being a loving person is messy, isn't it?" I had never thought of it that way, but after pondering that idea for a few days, I thought this: Love is messy, and hopefully, it can be wonderfully messy like Julie Andrew's Maria, in *Sound of Music*. The military officer, father of the Von Trapp family, loved his children, but believed that he must demand a certain kind of rigid behavior that tied them up in inhumane knots. Maria managed to make a "mess" of all that—with joy, spontaneity, song, and laughter. Any time we attempt to reinforce a rigid system, whether it is in marriage, family, business, religion, or politics, we dehumanize others and ourselves.

Unfortunately, the wonderful-messy loving family is too rare. Too many are default messy—the parents love their children but were never taught how to be creatively and joyfully loving, so they bumble along and raise children who get married and repeat the pattern. The default family, bad as it is, is better than the chaotic mess in which parents have been hurt so badly in their own childhood that they turn out to be mean and criminally hurtful to their children. They have a twisted belief that if they are being harsh with their children, they will turn out differently than they did. They falsely believe these children will be happier than they were and are. For centuries, these kinds of parents could continue their mean-spirited way with impunity. Wives and children were considered the *property* of the husband-father. Fortunately, that happens less often because it is against the law in all developed countries.

I grew up in the default messy-loving family. Looking back, I am sure that my parents loved each other and they loved us children, but poverty and ignorance got in the way of creating a life-giving messy family.

OPPOSITES DO ATTRACT

Marriage starts off being messy as we tend to choose our temperamental opposites. In 1911, when my parents married, they were temperamentally quite different, but what brought about the marriage was social pressure. Mom was pregnant at age fifteen, and in those days, the male sperm donor was expected to marry the woman—ready or not. And love or not. Thus, the saying, "shotgun wedding." In this marriage the temperamental opposite was incidental. Mom called the Hanley clan "shanty Irish." When I asked what her family was, she turned up her nose in mock *stuckupishness* and replied, "Lace-curtain Irish," and smiled rather delightfully.

Another word for temperamental could be personality type or the natural tendency, to be: outgoing and comfortable in most settings; or shy and introspective; or be moved more by emotions than thoughts; or always thinking and maybe let the feelings come, and so on—with a wide variety of ways of expressing ourselves. Sometimes the explorer type, who likes outdoor sports and risk-taking adventures, will choose a similar type as his or her partner—usually because that is how they met.

The majority of couples I have worked with in marriage counseling were opposites. An example of the opposites is the vivacious woman marrying the very serious and responsible man. He says: "I fell in love with her because she was so exciting and fun."

She says: "I fell in love with him because I felt so safe and secure with him."

When this couple comes in for marriage counseling, she is no longer vivacious; she is "volcanic," according to the husband. He is no longer solid and safe; he is emotionally unavailable and a "stick-in-the-mud."

Too often we marry our temperamental opposite and then spend the rest of our married life trying to make him or her just like us. What we need to do is accept our partners as we did at the beginning, and encourage minor changes. I once worked with a couple in which the wife enjoyed plays and the theater, and the husband loved sports. They decided to take turns attending events that the other liked.

edaniel
zulueta

She began to root for her favorite sports teams, and he began to look forward to plays. Another couple decided to get divorced and a few months later, the husband came in to see me about some personal issues. He was dressed completely different from the way he was when he came in with his wife. He wore a nice sports coat, nice shirt and slacks, and reported that he and his new "main squeeze" went dancing two or three times a week and, "Well, Doc, I've changed."

I was tempted to say, "Hey, dummy, your wife always wanted you to do these things."

I didn't say that though, because I was sure he already knew that. If he or she becomes mean and hurtful, then their ways of expressing themselves is beyond temperament and is dangerous. If this is the case, then separation is in order. In my experience, it is never helpful to stay together "for the sake of the children." The children are better off with separate parents than unhappy and angry parents in the same house.

One family attorney stated it this way, "It is better for the children to live with divorced parents, than with bickering parents." Nor should we stay together because we vowed "until death do us part." I hope you agree that a loving God would not want that. Most communities now have protective shelters for women and children who must flee from a harmful husband and father. Sometimes, it can be the wrathful mother. In either case, it is not shameful to call the police in situations like this.

OUR PARENTS ARE OUR MODELS FOR MARRIAGE

I don't know how many times I have been talking to a counselee and she or he tells me what they said to their partner and then, slapping a hand over their mouth, add, "Oh, my god, I sound just like my mother (or father)." It is to be expected, for after all, we lived with them for eighteen or more years. Young children soak in emotions, thoughts, and words like sponges. It would be wonderful if our parents accepted each other and us just as we are and encouraged us to develop our strengths in every area: physically, emotionally, intellectually, and spiritually. And, of course, they never put us down or ever used discouraging words. I have never met any parents like these, but I have known couples in which one had grown up in a positive "messy" family where laughter, singing, and joking came easily. If the partner's family had been stern and rigid, it was the stern partner who needed to "lighten up." Even if our family and/or parents were nearly perfect, we would have to find fault with them in order to separate ourselves from them and create our own separate lives.

I can recall only a few couples who said that they wanted a marriage as good as their parents. Most wanted to improve on the model their parents presented. They wanted to be more affectionate, respectful, financially secure, and so on. If they communicated well before the wedding, they vowed to be sensitive, kind, and intimate in all ways when they got married. If they are fortunate, they manage to be and do most of these things, except when it is "crunch time." Crunch time is when, seemingly, things fall apart—we get angry with one another, almost violently disagree on something, question one another like never before and seem near divorce. This is the time when our unconscious learning comes into play. We act like our parents by lashing out verbally and physically, say things we later regret, or walk away. This is the time we need to remember that we vowed to one another, or at least to ourselves, not to do all these things, and again make steps to change and reconnect with our partner.

CHANGE AS OPENING AND BECOMING MORE OF WHO WE ARE

Often, when our partner criticizes us or corrects us, we feel that he or she wants us to be someone else. There is a good couples book with the title *Do I Have to Give up Being Me to Be Loved by You?* that expresses this fear quite well. A better way to look at change is to use the example of a rosebud. When the rosebud grows and changes it becomes a fully blossoming rose. It does not become a tulip or some other flower. Usually our partner does not want us to become someone else, but it often feels that way. And it doesn't mean that our partner thinks he or she is perfect either, but when we were children, we thought our parents spoke for God. Sometimes, unfortunately, some parents thought that too.

We change, or blossom, by getting in touch with our *story*—the script we grew up with, and changing the feelings and thoughts that have tended to distance us from our partners. If my story growing up made me feel that one or both parents didn't like or love me, then I need to own that part of my story and amend it. The fact that my parents neglected me and showed it by criticizing me and yelling at me does not necessarily mean that my partner's criticisms—even the loud ones—are indicative that she doesn't like or love me. When our partner criticizes us, rather than sulking or yelling back, it might be helpful to ask, "When you said that (or yelled that) did you mean that you do not like or love me?"

A bad response would be, "Well, that's just the way I am, and you can like it or lump it." This last one was a common saying around my family when I was growing up.

Another model of change that focuses on changing habits looks something like this. It takes four steps to change a habit. Let us use an example of giving hugs to our partner—something my growing-up family never did:

1. Recognize the habit of just not even thinking of giving a hug.
2. The awkward state—"It's just not me." I give a hug but remain stiff and aloof. This is the step that usually ends the experience because we don't like feeling awkward or making changes.
3. I get pretty good at it but need to remind myself to do it. I relax and enjoy a hug, but still have to *remind* myself.
4. I gain a new habit. I find myself initiating a hug often, especially when I leave the house or return.

One of the best things about living in this modern era is that we can choose the way we want to be married—within limits, of course. There is no way we are supposed to act as dictated by other people. If we live in a small, tight-knit community, we may feel pressured to act in certain ways, such as attending church regularly, keeping our hair short if you're a man and long if a woman, not getting boisterous, never crying if you're a man or boy, not doing yard work if you're a woman, and many more *shoulds* or *should-nots*. Fortunately, I believe, this kind of social pressure is lessening because of television and mobility of families.

One of the most challenging things about the times we now live in is that we are in a tumultuous period concerning the way men and women relate. A humorous look at this was in a comic strip which showed a couple walking down a sidewalk and the young woman says to her date, "You are a very kind and accepting and understanding kind of person." Second frame, "You are a gentle and sensitive man." Third frame, "I've never gone out with a man like you." Last frame, they are at her doorstep, "I'd invite you in if you weren't such a wimp."

For centuries, men were supposed to be strong, brave, and the breadwinner. Women were the ones who stayed home and took care of the children. See *Ozzie and Harriet* or *Leave It to Beaver,* and other older TV sitcoms. The gender roles were clearly defined, even if we did not like them.

During most of human history, and even now, about half of men shielded the women in their world. Men were out hunting, fishing, or fighting by the sword while women remained with the clan—relating to one another and to the children. In the last hundred years, especially in developed countries, men have been asked to relate on a day-to-day basis in a way similar to the way women relate. Women have evolved as

relational and nurturing persons, while men have evolved as protectors and providers.

As women have moved into the workplace, their naturally developed relational skills often serve them well—especially when they are in leadership positions. Some, unfortunately, use these skills to manipulate people just as men have done. Also, unfortunately, some women believe they must drop all their ability for bringing loving kindnesses into a workplace, and become *macho* alpha bosses. Just as men enhance their lives and skills by incorporating some nurturing and relational abilities, women can enhance their skills by being more assertive but not aggressive.

I, personally, have had a difficult time letting go of the *dominant male* syndrome. Growing up in a father-dominated household and living alone with my dad for three years before he died when I was fourteen, left a heavy imprint on my mind-brain epigenetic habitual self. Because of my mother's depression and inability to make decisions, I became the head-of-the-house from fifteen on. My two youngest sisters would dispute that, but that is the story that determined my behavior. So Anne has had to put up with my feeble attempts to be less *macho* and more domesticated for all these years.

Owning Our Faults And Shortcomings

In our family, only my youngest sister escaped the habit of anesthetizing ourselves with alcohol. This added to the stubborn and independent bossiness we all seemed to have. I tried to fool myself into thinking my drinking was milder and less disabling than that of my siblings, but one of our daughters called me out, saying, "Dad, you were an out-of-control alcoholic and we were all scared of you when you were drinking." Of course that was hard to hear and to accept, but I am glad that she had the courage to say that to me. Alcoholics Anonymous was very helpful to me in changing that habit. I believe it helped me to see that life is a continual series of challenges and change. Addictive behavior is often inherited and, like other genetic characteristics, it can be changed. The best way to change the behavior is to create a more comfortable and safe environment in our family and social lives.

PERCEPTION MOTIVATES BEHAVIOR

We react to our perception of reality, not reality itself. If I think my wife is mad at me, then I react as if she is, whether or not she really is upset with me. Maybe it's the look on her face that reminds me of my dad's look when he was angry, or some other unpleasant experience. I have been amazed at the way we adults continue to react to others in the same, or similar, ways we did as children. It is helpful for us to ask ourselves, "Why did I do that, or say that?" Healthy introspection is necessary for personal growth. Unhealthy perceptions usually put the most negative slant on the experience.

I have often observed how differently my wife Anne and I react to situations. I think of the experiment mentioned in my first psychology course. The experimenters put thirty kittens into two cages. One cage had horizontal bars and the other had vertical bars. After six months, the experimenters exchanged the cats and cages so that the cats in the cage with horizontal bars were put in the cage with the vertical bars, and vice versa. The cats kept running into the bars in their new cages. They did not *see* the new bars, because they were conditioned to see only the bars they grew up with. This is a radical example of why we have different perceptions about the same things.

Sometimes our different conditioning can destroy a marriage if we do not examine it and change it. An example could be the wife growing up in an obsessively clean house where "cleanliness was next to godliness," and the husband grew up in one where messiness was tolerated and was not a big deal. Or he grew up in a home where one is expected to visit relatives often and without fail; she sees relatives as toxic and to be avoided. If either partner insists that his or her beliefs and habits are absolutely correct, there will be obvious problems. Compromises are often necessary for the sake of love and the marriage.

When working with a couple in counseling, I often ask each of the partners how they reacted to their parents—especially to the parent of the opposite gender. If you, the husband, were very close to your mother, you might find it easy to be close to your wife. Or you might find yourself constantly criticizing your wife for not being more like your mother. If your mother was smothering in her closeness, you might become almost phobic to closeness and unconsciously push your wife away. If you, the wife, were afraid of your father, you might find yourself overly afraid of your husband, especially when you have disagreed on something.

I have noticed that people tend to become either very similar to one or both parents, or work hard to be the opposite. For example, I decided to never be angry like my dad, and I may have succeeded, but I did hit each of my daughters when I was angry, drinking, and in my own *crunch time*. Some people grow up in an alcoholic family and become alcoholics themselves while one or more of their siblings become rigid teetotalers. There are so many ways we are influenced by our parents and relatives, often absorbing their actions and attitudes like sponges, and we don't give it a thought until we get married and start interacting with our spouse's kin the same way our family members did.

If a man's father seemed distant from his mother and the children, he may, as a husband and father, mimic his father by "marrying" his work and/or profession. If the wife's mother doted on her children and ignored her father, the wife may do the same. It is very important that we *decide* how best to create the kind of marriage we want, and not just fall into a pattern because that is the way we observed around us when we were growing up. Too often we find ourselves being bossy, controlling, over-possessive, cold, smothering, and more, and never examine the underlying reasons until we find our marriage falling apart.

ON SUBSTANCE ABUSE AND ADDICTIONS

There is an epidemic of alcoholism and substance abuse in our country right now. The success of marriage is often dependent upon the way the addicted person handles the addiction. There is a tendency for addictions to be inherited. Note that I said "tendency" because if it runs in a family, it does not mean that a person will naturally become an addict or alcoholic. With self-discipline a person can avoid it and if he or she is "hooked," he or she can recover from it. Alcoholics Anonymous and other twelve-step programs can be very helpful. I agree with these programs that state that we are not sober until we have been sober for at least one year—and have passed holidays, anniversaries, successes and failures, and all of life's natural ups and downs, and have not drunk any alcohol nor taken any mind-altering drugs. If we start a program and "fall off the wagon," look at it as a lapse and not a complete failure. We can pick up the pieces and try again.

If you are the spouse of an alcoholic, show emotional support in every way possible, except by providing the alcohol or drugs. If he or she is working a rehab program, please don't say, "Oh, you'll never change. That's just the way you are!" If you have already done this, apologize and start over. The Al Anon program can be wonderfully helpful to the spouse and other family members of an alcoholic person. I believe that stopping an addictive habit is one of the most difficult and courageous actions any person can take. As with all change, say to yourself, "Others have done it and are doing it, so I can too."

Life's Stages And Marriage

Hopefully, we become more mature and wiser as we get older. Unfortunately, we often do not, or think we cannot, change in some areas of our life that would enhance our lives—especially our marital and family life. In graduate school, I had a delightful professor who said that there are three adolescent periods in life:

1. Infancy to childhood—the so-called "terrible twos"—or explosive and inquisitive twos, threes, and fours.

2. Childhood to adulthood—the period we usually think of as Adolescence, from age 14 through the teen years or early twenties.

3. Adulthood to maturity—or discovery of one's True Self—including the mid-life crisis occurring sometime between 35 and 50. As adults, we are often (perhaps too often) concerned with practical things—status, income, looks, place in society, etc, rather than on becoming more mature and loving. When we pass through the "third adolescence," we become more concerned with our emotional and spiritual growth and the closeness of our relationships with others (and with our God or spiritual lives).

My professor, Dr. Bernard Boelen, contended that only a minority of men and women really go through the difficult

process or period of level 3—adulthood to maturity or being their *true selves*. When they do, he or she becomes more generous, hospitable, friendly, caring, and compassionate. He or she easily shares what they have. Their actions declare, "My humanity is intrinsically bound up with yours," and "a person is a person through other people. I am a human because I belong. I participate. I share."

If we can embrace some of these sentiments, starting with our partnerships, we can enhance our lives, our community, and our world. Yes, I am an idealist and a hopeful person. Some might say, "A hopeful idiot," and that is okay, but I would not want to change my position on that. Marriage can be our way of fully entering into the social life of our planet.

DISCUSSION POINTS

- *Describe the defenses you developed in your family of origin. If, hopefully, you are reading this with your partner, share your thoughts—AND do not discourage one another by emphasizing faults.*

- *Who were your teachers who helped you most in becoming a caring and loving person? What films or books were most helpful to you?*

- *What are some of the best things you have learned since you have been in this relationship?*

- *What would you like to learn from your partner?*

- *What are some areas your partner would like for you to change? How could he or she help you?*

Chapter 3

ON COMMUNICATION

Communication is the largest single factor determining what kinds of relationships she or he makes with others and what happens to each in the world.

Virginia Satir

Virginia Satir, one of the pioneers in Family Therapy, goes on to say: "How we manage survival, how we develop intimacy, how productive we are, how we make sense, how we connect with our own divinity— all depend largely on our communication skills." I had the good fortune to spend several days and hours with Virginia and I can attest to the fact that she is one of the best communicators I've ever met or observed in person, film, books, or audio tapes and CDs. She was present—physically; you could see it in her eyes and she would make sure she was within touching distance if it was a conversation. She was present emotionally; you could feel her warmth. She was present mentally; she brought her excellent mind/brain into action so that she was always interested. She made contact and you knew it.

Over the years, it seems that the majority of couples I've seen in marriage therapy say: "We just don't communicate." What they usually mean is that they seldom make contact with one another, or that the kind of contact they do make creates distance rather than closeness. We are *always* communicating if we live with one another. If we are in an intimate relationship, we spend time with one another and remain quiet; it is often because we are very comfortable together and so we do not need to talk all the time. Or it could mean that *I think I cannot talk to you without you getting angry.* Or it could mean that *I really don't care—but we are communicating* _something_. Sometimes couples add "anymore" to "we don't communicate," because at one time they did communicate, or they believe that they did.

How do we know whether or not we are making contact with another person? Sometimes it is because we know that the other person is really listening to us—that is, making eye contact and tuning in to what we have to say. It is as if he or she is really trying to understand not only what we are saying, but also what we are experiencing or have experienced. Usually we just know when we are making contact with other people. We know this because at other times, people merely look at us or glance in our direction, but do not see us.

When I saw the film *Chicago,* I was struck by the song, *Mr. Cellophane*. It went something like this: "Cellophane, Mr. Cellophane, shoulda been my name, Mr. Cellophane, 'cause you look right through me, walk right by me, and never know I'm there." It struck me, first, because that was the way I felt as a child in my dysfunctional family, and second, because I realized that many husbands and wives frequently feel that way in their own marriages and families. Husbands feel that way when they come home and find their wives and children busy doing something and might say, "Hi," and continue doing whatever it is they are doing and ignore the new arrival in the house. Of course, it could be the wife coming home. Here's another example: When you, as a couple, go into a restaurant, notice the other couples. You can nearly always pick out the ones who are married and the ones who are not. Many, if not most, married couples look bored, glumly looking past each other, whereas, the non-married couples are animatedly discussing something and looking directly at each other.

Those glum married couples once had the same interest in one another as their more animated, unmarried counterparts. I remember paying attention to every word Anne said before we were married and for the first few years afterwards. Just as I now know there are things

I am interested in and she is not, so we just avoid those topics and our interests often lags. It took several years to realize that we stopped *making as much contact* as before so I began to deliberately start talking about subjects I knew she was interested in. One of the partners needs to find ways to reconnect when we notice it is missing. Take a few minutes and discuss this with your partner. If you still go to restaurants and look into each other's eyes and notice the sparkle in your spouse's gaze, then you can ignore the suggestion to discuss this.

In fact, if you still do this, you probably aren't reading this book.

THE FIVE LOVE LANGUAGES

For some answers, I recommend that you obtain a copy of Gary Chapman's small book, *The Five Love Languages*. The author gives us a helpful idea that each of us has a primary way that we wish to show our love to our partner. The five are:

1. **Giving gifts**: You may like giving gifts but your partner may not. If this is the case, he or she may just casually drop the gift on a chair, unconsciously dismissing you. Don't assume your partner doesn't care, and bring up the idea of how gift-giving is so important to you.

2. **Sharing quality time**: Your partner may like the talk you have *about* the gift more than the gift you gave. So you have a less expensive way of giving her a "gift." There is no *love language* that is better than another. He/she is not stupid because she likes time with you more than a diamond bracelet.

3. **Words of affirmation**: This is also a favorite of mine— probably because I received so few encouraging words when I was young. And it is important to note that if

your partner likes quality time or gifts more than words of affirmation, telling him or her, "You know I love you, babe," won't cut it.

4. **Acts of service:** This is definitely my wife's favorite: "Give me a good foot rub, and I'll follow you anywhere." It could be anything out of the ordinary. When I was first married, I wanted Anne to notice when I did the dishes and to thank me for it. It took me a year to realize that it was just one chore I needed to do because I didn't like to cook. So, for 45 years, I have been the chief dishwasher– and don't expect some kind of *attaboy*.

5. **Physical touch or physical intimacy:** Hundreds of times, I have heard female partners comment that their male counterparts want sex every time they give them a casual hug or kiss. Having sex is wonderful and life-giving, and so is just giving and receiving hugs and kisses with no expectations.

Each of us tend to give what we most enjoy receiving, so we have the challenge to discover what our partner likes best. I believe these "languages" are an important set of ideas for every couple and does go well with the development of our verbal communication.

FOUR BARRIERS TO EFFECTIVE COMMUNICATION

The famous couples researcher, John Gottman, tells us there are four distinct ways or attitudes that we use to avoid real contact in communication. He calls them the Four Horsemen: criticism, contempt, defensiveness, and stonewalling. Each is a method of encouraging our partner to find it more difficult to make contact with us and to enhance our relationship.

Criticism is Gottman's first horseman. Here are some examples: "The trouble with you is you're so stupid." Or "You're nuts, just like the rest of your family," or "Don't you know how to do anything right?" The trouble with criticism is that it simply hurts too much. I remember the first time Anne criticized me in our early years of marriage. It felt like I was a vulnerable child again and being scolded by one of my mean-spirited siblings. I wondered what happened to this wonderful person I had married. A critical comment from the partner hurts a thousand times more than if it was said by someone else. Our partner, we believe, is the one who loves us deeply and forever.

As the seventh of eight children, I received criticisms by the bucketful, so I am very sensitive when it comes to criticism. Anne, knowing how sensitive I am, usually precedes any remark that can be interpreted as criticism by saying, "Just an observation, not a criticism." One of Gottman's findings, after studying over 3,000 couples, was this: Positive couples, who have stayed together happily for up to 20 years or more, would give five compliments or appreciations to every one zinger, even when they were fighting. And the ratio of compliments to criticism was 20 to 1 during regular times. What are you aware of with your partner? Do your expressions of appreciation outnumber your criticisms?

Criticism often leads to the second horseman, **Contempt.** We've all heard the old saying that "familiarity breeds contempt" and this is too often true in marriage. If this is one of your more familiar attitudes towards your partner, it is important to take a look at it. The dictionary defines contempt as "losing respect or reverence for someone or something." It conveys disgust rather than caring and respect. Hopefully, you only dislike some aspect or habit of your partner, but don't hold contempt toward him or her as a person. When I find myself directing any kind of contempt toward Anne, I quickly remind myself of how I felt before we were married and were deeply in love. I try to call up that feeling almost instantly and nip my negativity in the bud.

It is helpful to find out why you dislike something your partner habitually does. It you hated your father because of his abusive ways, it is easy to transfer that attitude or feeling onto your partner when he even hints at being harsh or abusive. Let your partner know how you feel, first, because he shouldn't talk or act that way, and second, he reminds you of your father.

Of course, it is important to take notice of your own manner of speaking. If it is contemptuous in any way, it adds fuel to the fire—and your partner becomes even more contemptuous toward you.

Maybe you, the husband, had a mother, stepmother, ex-wife or girlfriend, who acted or talked in what you consider a cheap or obnoxious way, and you have transferred how that made you feel toward your current partner. Often, it is *lack* of familiarity that breeds contempt; we really don't know our partners well enough. We don't know what they have experienced that makes them lash out like they do. Let your partner know you! It is absolutely necessary to get past contempt if you wish to have a loving marriage.

Defensiveness is the third way to put an emotional barrier between you and your partner. This habit is the one with which I have had the most difficulty. I believe it is because of the rather constant criticism I received as a child in my unhappy family of origin. I felt like I had to constantly defend myself. As we look over our personal history, we will often find that, as adults, we often automatically react to our partner the way we did to family members when we were children. So, if someone says something critical or even something that could remotely be construed as critical, I may have reacted like this: "What the hell is the matter with you? Why are you so thin-skinned?" So I add another criticism to the one I have already laid on. I might have said, "Well, you aren't so damn perfect yourself!" And so the escalation begins, the argument heats up, and we don't live happily ever after. I eventually learned to make better responses, like: "Please say that again, in a way that will help me understand what you mean." Or, "Did you really intend to put me down?" or some other non-defensive remark—in a non-defensive tone of voice, of course.

Remember that we grew up learning to communicate in certain ways, and many of them are not helpful in building a close, life-giving relationship. When working with couples, I often point out how harsh comments, criticism, and defensive remarks hurt the relationship. The offending partner frequently responds that he or she is much softer and easier than his or her parents are or were. Even though you might be "better than" your father or mother, doesn't mean that you do not need improvement in your marriage. Sometimes people's defenses are so strong that their partners just cannot get through to them, no matter how hard they try.

The defensive person has worked on the defensive posture since childhood, and it has become part of them. The only way to get through to that person is to help them realize the difficulty you are having and, hard as it is to do, accept that person where he or she is, and keep working. Often, couples counseling can help.

Stonewalling, the fourth horseman, can be stubbornly holding on to the same position, or just walking away and not responding at all. This latter is, perhaps, the most common, and is learned in childhood to protect oneself from further hurt from a parent or other family member. Stonewalling and defensiveness frequently go together. An example of this would be a person who has learned to totally defend themselves in such a way that no suggestions, criticisms, and even emotion expressed by others seem to penetrate their defensive boundaries. I call this the "fortress defense." It is a very safe way to live because the person does not let anyone bother them. The downside is that the person is very lonely and sometimes depressed, because not only do others' words or feelings not penetrate their defenses, but they cannot allow their verbal and emotional expressions to go out to anyone else. That person is usually puzzled as to why his wife or husband seems to be so distant.

They appear not to care, so those who would otherwise be close drift away and stop trying to connect.

Stonewalling is probably the strongest and toughest of all the horsemen. The stonewaller cannot be budged unless he or she wishes to be budged. Stonewallers may say that they just cannot stand confrontations of any kind. In reality, they are excellent at handling confrontations—they become impenetrable fortresses. If you are one of these people, and you wish to have a life-giving marriage, let your partner know that you believe that this is your defense, and ask your partner to keep trying, and to let you know when you seem untouchable or distant. If I, the husband, use this stonewalling defense, I may believe that talk is useless and sexual intimacy is the only kind of real intimacy. The stonewaller is completely puzzled why their partner refuses to have sex.

Usually a person develops this kind of pattern in childhood—to defend oneself from harsh, alcoholic or absent parents. We all, unfortunately, need defenses; otherwise we get bulldozed by the people and world around us. What is important is that our defenses serve to protect us when needed. When they emerge automatically against a loved one, they create barriers to emotional intimacy and healthy communication.

FOUR DESTRUCTIVE AND ONE GOOD WAY TO COMMUNICATE

Virginia Satir says that there are four toxic ways of talking to one another in marriages, families, and other partnerships. They are: Placating, Blaming, Being Super-Reasonable, and Distracting. And there is **ONE** positive way: being direct. By *direct*, I mean saying what you are really thinking and feeling. It is not, as many people claim, saying whatever they like, in any damn way they please. They might blurt out, "You are so damn stupid, and I say that because I'm pretty damn direct." In my view (and Virginia's), a person like that is not direct, nor interested in making contact with another, but is merely insensitive and hurtful.

Let's take a look at the four toxic, or negative, ways to communicate. **Placating.** Placators have a habit of putting themselves down or discounting themselves— and consequently feeling angelic because they have been so "nice." Placators make good partners for blamers, because they will avoid arguments by saying something like, "Whatever you say, dear," and often follow it with a passive-aggressive tendency to do whatever they like—which widens the gap between the partners. The placator may transform into a blamer and throw back some blame, and the argument continues.

Blaming is easy to identify and recognize as devilish: Whenever something goes wrong, it is your fault (or anyone's fault except mine, the speaker). He or she (or me) will let you know   about it by making loud blaming remarks. The blamer is very good at putting his or her partner on the defensive. It is a great way to avoid intimacy and hurt your partner.

The **super-reasonable** person will give an analysis of the "problem" usually in a condescending tone of voice that implies you are quite stupid for thinking the way you do. For example: "Here is the problem. When you do the dishes, you waste water by letting it run too long

while you are rinsing them before putting them in the dishwasher. I have estimated that it takes fourteen extra gallons of water per month and costs us 89 cents per month. Now if you …" Personally, I'd rather be yelled at. This style is common for the stonewalling-defensive persons mentioned earlier.

The funny partner is the **distracter.** Say you are in a real tizzy about your partner spending $200 on an item that is a budget-buster and which you perceive as completely unnecessary. So you say, in an upset tone of voice, "I thought that we agreed not to spend any unnecessary money this month." The distracter responds. "You know, honey, you are really cute when you're angry—your face is such a nice shade of pink!" Of course you take a deep breath, and put down the butcher knife.

The single positive method for communicating, **being direct,** sounds easy but actually isn't.

Direct communication means saying what you are thinking and feeling, clearly and without placating, blaming, super-reasoning, or distracting. I often notice that one or both partners are unclear about what they feel or think, and they try using "direct" wording while still blaming. An example of blaming disguised as directness would sound something like this, "I think you are being real stupid when you talk like that." Using the overspending example mentioned above, a truly direct approach would be something like this, "You know, Harry, we agreed that we would not spend money on any unnecessary things this month. I am really upset that you spent $200 on that new jacket." This clearly expresses what the wife thinks and feels. Learning to speak directly takes a great deal of effort, time, and practice, because usually we are working to overcome a lifetime of poor communication habits. And the habits often go back to childhood when we were observing our own parents and relatives.

Many years ago I worked with a couple, and the wife was close to filing for divorce because her husband teased her relentlessly (he was a distracter). When I saw the husband alone, I asked him about his constant teasing. After a bit of exploration regarding his family of origin, he realized that teasing was the most common way to communicate among the eight children in his family. I realized, for the first time, that we had used the same method of communication in our large family.

Learning To Fight Fair

Direct communication is an important part of learning to fight fair. To put it another way, we must learn the art of gentle confrontation. Gottman states that happy couples need to have *successful repair attempts*; that is, they must learn to reconnect after disconnecting during the arguments. In his book, *The Intimate Enemy*, George Bach states that every couple *needs to* fight in order to resolve problems, rather than have those problems go underground and become roadblocks in developing a loving relationship. I agree that we need to fight, but we must learn to fight fairly—to confront our partners gently rather than aggressively.

We usually think of confrontation as a battle between enemies or antagonists. But you can be a gentle confronter, or a fair fighter, and learn to solve problems in a way that draws you closer to your partner. Here are some rules for fair fighting from George Bach's book:

First we must fight for *understanding*, and not in order to hurt one another. Second, work hard *not to intentionally hurt;* that is, don't blame, condemn, or bring up things from the past, but rather focus on the present issue. Third, *don't fight when you are angry,* but make an "appointment" to resolve your problems. If, in spite of applying the above points, you end up with real argument, remember that things said in the heat of battle are very emotionally laden, and usually regretted later. They should be allowed to be washed away by the next wave of emotions—like a wave erases messages written in the sand. That's why it is important not to fight when we are angry.

One wife said, "We never fought before, but we were growing further and further apart. Now that we have learned how to fight, we get along better. It's like we had to feel safe with one another in order to fight to resolve our differences.

A MODEL FOR GENTLE CONFRONTATION

I recommend a model of confrontation that Anne and I learned in our first year of marriage, an idea from Harvey Jackins' co-counseling model of communication. In this model, the couple sits facing one another (knees touching, or nearly so) and give each other three minutes to state their views on some problem or topic about which they disagree. Then put a clock nearby so that they can time themselves. One partner takes the first three minutes and states his or her ideas on the subject, and the partner listens. It is important to look at each other and recall how you felt when you were dating; think of the warm feelings you had then. The listening partner shows they are listening by keeping eye contact and not interrupting; the listening partner waits for their turn to speak. Even if the speaking partner is not finished at the end of three minutes, he or she stops speaking and becomes the listener.

It is amazing how quickly you can solve a problem when you give each other your undivided attention and do not interrupt each other. Notice how every argument escalates quickly because of the interruptions. A couple can usually solve a problem with three six-minute rounds—each person has three minute sessions—to explain his or her ideas or positions. Of course, the couple needs to follow the above suggestions on direct communication.

Each person needs to be familiar with their customary pattern of verbal "combat." For example: One person usually wants to settle the problem RIGHT NOW and cannot wait. Of course, he or she can wait but believes that they *cannot* wait—because that has been their habit. To become a successful problem solver—or marriage partner—we need to know and practice that we can change our habits if it is helpful to the partnership.

It is important not to *gunny sack*—keep little problems, grievances, and resentments in a mental gunny (burlap bag) sack, and then, when one last straw breaks your resolve, dump the contents onto your partner, like this: "And not only did you get that stop-sign ticket, but last week you also nearly ran that Ford off the road when we were coming home, and before that, you let the car run of gas and we had to call AAA, and last month, you dinged the rear fender backing out of Target!" All of this is said in an angry, contemptuous tone of voice. Ask yourself if that is the message you want to give to the person you profess to love dearly, or is your devil doing the talking?

Another very important point in communication is to stay in the *now* when talking with your partner—don't think about the project you are working on, how stupid your partner is, or some other distraction that takes you away from the conversation. Stay in contact with your partner. Notice their tone of voice, words, facial expressions, meaning, and, well, everything about them and what they are saying.

MAKE YOUR RELATIONSHIP *I-THOU*, NOT *I-IT*

Keeping good communication includes meaningful contact by being *I-Thou* with our partner as recommended by Martin Buber, whom I mentioned in the first chapter. The I-Thou relationship is more personal, contact-full, and respectful of the other person's individuality and humanity.

Over the years of working with couples and families, I have noticed that the husband frequently relates to his wife in an *I-It* kind of way. It is a role-to-role encounter—a husband-to-wife connection rather than a Susan and Joe relationship. The husband talks to his wife and children in the same way that he talks to his employees. (Of course, it is best if he talks to his employees with more respect, too.) Or perhaps the wife talks to her husband or children as if they were servants, rather than the people she loves most in the world. Sometimes, during counseling sessions, I hear a man or woman say things like: "My partner left me standing …" and he is sitting right there next to her. I have heard men do the same thing. A life-giving relationship is always built on many I-Thou moments.

Another way to look at making contact is to tune in to our partner, like two tines or tuning-forks vibrating in harmony. She does not need to tell him that she is tired and needs help, because he sees it in her face and the way she moves—he *tunes in*. It takes a lot of asking and explaining before intimate partners become tuning forks.

DISCUSSION POINTS

- *How would you describe your customary way of communicating with your partner? What is your "favorite" modality—Placating, Blaming, being Super-reasonable, or Distracting? In a non-judgmental or antagonistic way, describe your partner's style—as you experience it.*

- *How would you describe the communication between your parents when you were growing up?*

- *What do you think of the idea that perception motivates our actions more than the objective reality? Can you think of an instance in your own experience that relates to the I-Thou concept?.*

- *What are a few of your favorite I-Thou moments with your partner? Will you share them with him or her? (Hopefully, again.)*

- *Which of the "four horsemen"—Criticism, Contempt, Defensiveness and Stonewalling—is your most common mode?*

- *Are you making real I-Thou contact with your partner as you discuss all this?*

- *What are some special ways your partner says "I love you"? Please tell him or her.*

Chapter 4

MONEY

When the power of love overcomes the love of power, the world will know peace ... (and more life-giving marriages)

Jimi Hendrix

The above quote from Jimi Hendrix is meaningful when we think of our culture, our relationships, and money. Money is one of the most contentious items in nearly all marriages and is the focus of this chapter. For centuries, many men have lorded it over their wives because they were the ones with the money—and therefore the ones with power. This has been changing as more and more women have gone into the workforce and states have passed community property laws, but the attitude remains prevalent. In my therapy practice, I have heard men argue with their wives about being entitled to do this or that because they make more money. Or, even more insidious, say, "If we get divorced, I'll see that you don't get a cent." Fortunately, some women know that they live in a community property state, and have the right to half of all the couple has earned since they have been married. The wives have earned it, even if they have never been employed outside the home—and most states recognize this. Unfortunately, there are still states that do not have community property laws.

MONEY REALLY CANNOT BUY HAPPINESS

Apart from the above, in our culture, we too often see money and material possessions as a source of prestige and power. We frequently mouth the phrase, "Money does not buy happiness," but we work hard to try to make it happen anyway. For nearly forty years, I have reflected on Abraham Maslow's theory about human motivation. He contends that we are motivated by our human needs, as opposed to the psychologists who believe that we are conditioned to act in a certain way and are thus not responsible for the choices we make because we have been programmed to make them. We may have grown up in poverty and decided to dedicate our lives to making as much money as possible—unlike our parents, who seemed content to live in poverty. I use the word "decided" deliberately, because I do believe it is a choice. Of course, our parents may have wanted to make more money and live in better circumstances, but because of circumstances—lack of education, illness, depression, etc.—could not.

Meeting Our Needs

Maslow theorized that we have five basic, or *deficiency* needs— needs which, if not met, make us deficient as persons—and they are:

1. Physical needs
2. Safety and security
3. Love and belonging
4. Self-esteem
5. Autonomy

Our *physical needs* are, of course, the most basic: air, water, food, and, depending on the climate, shelter for warmth or shade. For the starving person, paradise is a place where there is food. I believe we need to remind ourselves that the majority of humans on our little planet still do not have their physical needs adequately met—especially enough food.

Self-Actualizing Person
Using all personal
Potential

Being
Needs

Beauty Needs

Understanding and
Information Need

Respect and
Self-esteem Need

Deficiency
Needs

Belonging and
Love Need

Security
Need

Physical
Need

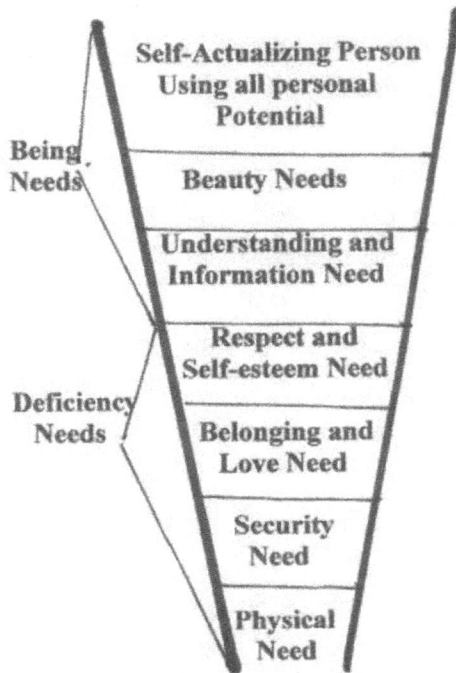

ABRAHAM MASLOW'S HIERARCHY OF NEEDS

Once our physical needs are met, we yearn to have these needs met on a safe and regular basis, thus, we have *safety and security needs.* The *autonomy,* or freedom, need weaves itself through the other needs; thus, a person may trade autonomy or freedom in order to have food or safety. A poor person may marry a rich person in order to have material possessions, safety and prestige, although sometimes the "good provider" is mean and hurtful. Or a person may remain at a dehumanizing job because they are afraid of not being able to provide for their family's basic needs if they quit.

I have often thought that *love and belonging* should be considered distinct needs because a person may join an organization, such as a religion that is very rigid, controlling, and anything but loving, in order to have a feeling of belonging. And this can be true of even a profession. Marilyn Monroe is quoted as saying, in answer to why she became an actress, "When you grow up thinking you are a nobody, you think that you need to become someone else in order to be somebody." Real love is more than just belonging—it is, ideally, a life-sharing relationship that allows us to develop all of our talents and gifts. Of course, marriage should fit into that category.

True love is the need that, if properly filled, will lead us to be able to fill the next basic need—*self-esteem*. Because we often find it so difficult to develop this dynamic love, we may settle for attempting to gain esteem by having a snazzy car, large house, maybe even a boat—and if we really have very great self-esteem, we may own a yacht. If you did not chuckle, at least a little, with that last remark, you are completely missing what I'm saying. How else can we explain why a couple will tie themselves down to a house payment that they can barely afford in order to live in a house with a four-car garage and 4,000 square feet of living space for their family of three?

I truly believe that we U.S. citizens have, as a culture, tried (unconsciously) to jump over love and belonging in an attempt to obtain self-esteem—to gain it with the prestige that comes from material possessions. I once worked with a young man who had just graduated from a prestigious university, but was heart-broken because his sweetheart, whom he hoped to marry, had just dropped him. She did this after he told her that he was going to graduate school to become a social worker. She informed him that he could never make enough money as a social worker to make her happy. I encouraged him to think that she had given him a gift, because, in my thinking, if she was that shallow, she would have been very difficult to please throughout their lives together—no matter what he did for a living or how much money he made. And, of course, I mentioned that it was not possible for one person to *make* another person happy. Ironically, we can do a pretty good job of making them miserable, but we can't make them happy.

WE'RE CONDITIONED TO THINK ABOUT MONEY
IN A CERTAIN WAY

Back to being conditioned: We are at least swayed, if not determined, by our upbringing, and I would like to share a little of my own experience about money. As mentioned before, I spent six of my early years—ages 11 though 16—in the very small town of Edgemont, South Dakota. We were poor and I had to work to buy my own clothes, go to the movies, get candy, and so on. If I had an extra nickel, I would buy myself a Snickers after lunch as I walked back to school. I had the extra nickel about once every two weeks. I remember thinking that, when I grew up, I'd have enough money to buy a Snickers whenever I wanted one. In my mid-thirties, I was standing at the checkout line at a drug store and looking at the candy stand. I had the thought, *I wish I could afford to buy a Snickers.* And then I said to myself, "Damn it, I *can* afford to buy a Snickers. What have I been thinking?"

This is a good example of how we often carry old beliefs into our adult lives, without giving a thought to where those beliefs came from. In my case, I grew up thinking that we just had barely enough to get by, but never enough to buy extras. The family did not own a car until I was fourteen years old, and then it was an eight-year-old used car. We had a telephone in the house only three of my first fourteen years of life. Interestingly, though, I never felt like we were poor because we usually had a small but clean rented house and enough to eat (even if it was the same stew we had Monday, Tuesday, and Wednesday). And, more importantly, most of the people in the small towns we lived in were in very similar circumstances. After all these years, I still need to be aware that my habitual way of thinking is: We only have barely enough to get by and no matter how much we spend, we'll still get by, but only barely. One thing that was very positive was our parents' rather constant reminder that we were not *poor white trash*, so we must always mind our manners and study and work hard. Although I am the only one of the eight children to attend college, all were hard workers. "Nobody can say that a Hanley is not a hard worker. Nobody!" was our family motto. We might give away our hard work for too low a wage, but we worked hard.

edaniel
zulueta

Now, if I had married a woman who expected lots of extravagant things and for whom shopping was a major vocation, we would have been in deep trouble. Fortunately, I married Anne, who gets great joy in finding a bargain on anything she buys. (Hmmm...I wonder if she was thinking *bargain* when she agreed to marry me? I think she got more than she bargained for! Hopefully, more good than bad.)

So when we talk about money with our partners, we need to consider our own background and, perhaps, question the values and beliefs with which we have grown up. In my experience, men are more likely than women to tie their sense of self-worth into their financial success. Of course, there are many exceptions. When a couple is forced into bankruptcy or other kinds of financial trouble, the man most often feels like a complete failure and the wife is just worried about how they are going to buy the groceries. "My worth as a person is not dependent on my income," is a saying I used in my counseling for years until a time came when, due to a very poor investment in a graduate school, we had to declare bankruptcy. I became very deeply depressed, while Anne was just concerned about keeping the house and paying for our girls' college expenses. I was a *failure*, while she just had some financial problems. The reverse can be true, too, with some couples.

What Is Success in Life?

Of course, it is helpful if both of you, as a couple, can talk about how you view money, property, and what each of you believes constitutes "success." Hopefully, your idea of success is not tied to how much money you make or have or what kind of material possessions you own. If you are not yet married, I encourage you to talk, in depth, about these things. And I hope you will use the ideas we discussed in the last chapter regarding communication. Over forty years ago, I wrote this on a greeting card: "No matter what great things a man may do in life, unless he becomes a loving person, his life is a failure." After working with hundreds of couples in therapy, I believe it even more today.

If you live on a tight budget, it is important that you have an agreement as to how much you can spend without consulting your partner. When Anne and I were first married, that amount was $50. Later, we raised it to $100 and that has stayed with us over the years. This should be a *mutual* agreement—not an order given by one partner.

Some couples are content to have two checking accounts, and each has a certain responsibility to cover his or her share of household expenses.

I once worked with a couple whose central issue was money. They had four children and the mother was a full-time mother and homemaker. The husband made the decision to give his wife a certain monthly amount of money to cover household expenses: food, clothing, utilities, phone, entertainment, school supplies, etc. He automatically made the house payment, but she had to take care of all the rest. He had not shopped for groceries since they were married, and had never shopped for the children's clothes. The amount he allotted for her

expenses was impossibly low. Every week, she had to beg him for extra money, and he always wound up being scolded for being a spendthrift. She had endured this for years, for the children's sake, but finally said that if they did not get some counseling on this, she would file for divorce. Fortunately, they came for counseling and he was willing to learn and change or risk losing his family. Obviously, they really had some repair work to do. For starters, I insisted that he accompany her to the grocery store the next two weeks. And, of course, we had to work on her self-esteem and his *need* for power *over* her—displayed by the money issue. Remember this challenge: We need to be strong enough to have power *with*, and not power *over*, our partners!

DISCUSSION POINTS

- *What were some of your ideas and values regarding money when you were growing up? How have they changed over the years?*

- *How would you describe your parents' ideas about money and material things?*

- *How did your parents make decisions about purchasing "big-ticket" items, such as a house, cars, major appliances, etc.?*

- *How are your ideas different from your parents' ideas?*

- *How would you like to be able to talk with your partner about these things?*

- *Are gaining material possessions in any way getting in the way of your life-giving love toward one another? If so, how can you change it? Are the two of you on the same page on this subject?*

- *Do you equate financial well-being with success?*

- *If you could make it happen, what would you change about your lifestyle?*

Chapter 5

SEX, ATTENTION, ACCEPTANCE, APPROVAL, AND AFFECTION

"Sex is a sacrament—a sacred outward symbol of a spiritual reality."
Don Hanley

"Sex is procreative, communicative, natural, and fun."
Masters and Johnson

"If we don't have great sex, we don't have a great spiritual life."
Irwin Kula, from Jewish wisdom

All three of the above concepts are ideals and, I believe, true statements, but not commonly perceived that way, nor lived out in practice. I am convinced that if the thinkers of our Western world had worked hard to come up with a more tortuous, dysfunctional, and confusing set of teachings and attitudes toward human sexuality, they could not have done better than what we have been taught and now experience.

I am assuming that couples reading this booklet and discussing the ideas have been together long enough to be past the original falling in love and honeymoon stage—that wonderful stage in which the beloved could do no wrong—and you are now wondering, at least part of the time, *Why did I marry this character?* And you are now wondering how to reconnect and bridge the intimacy gap that has developed between the two of you. Many men believe that if they'd just make love more often, everything would be fine. Of the several hundred couples I've worked with, only one wife believed that more frequent sex was the answer. Even earlier in marriage, men are more apt to see sex as the real contact time between themselves and their wives—the cure-all for every disengagement. Sex is also the time when the man feels most united with his partner; he is *one with*, or truly sharing himself with, his significant other. Wives invariably want to have more intimate time—sharing, talking, doing other things together, and then letting sex be the climax of their time together, not the entirety of their intimate moments. Again, I recommend that the two of you look at the Five Love Languages recommended earlier.

edaniel
zulueta

Connecting And Passion

When trying to repair the intimate and the sexual gap between couples, I see two challenges:

1. Reconnecting
2. Renewing our passion

We do not need to wait until all problems are solved before renewing our lovemaking, but it needs to be done at least simultaneously as we learn better ways to connect in a positive way. Often both partners just don't feel close anymore. Wives feel that they are not respected and given enough power in the marriage and in the family, and that too much of the work of housekeeping and parenting falls on her. The husband avoids sex because he feels he has been rejected too many times, and now the children, or other interests, or both, are more important to her than he is. Each person has learned to find what pleasure they can experience in life elsewhere—their work, the children, hobbies. Or, more often than not, they have stopped feeling pleasure, period.

I am convinced that we are not a pleasure-seeking society, but rather a distraction-seeking society, because we've never learned how to truly enjoy sensual pleasure—sight (a sunset, paintings, scenery, etc.), sound (music, singing, playing an instrument), taste (good food and not just filling up on on-the-go food), smell (aromas that enhance), touch (massage, a hug, a caress, a bubble bath, and sex). So stop and look at, touch and smell the roses, and everything else that is beautiful—including your family members.

For Better Sex (and a More Pleasurable Life)

Some couples believe that it is impossible to have satisfying sex with a partner you have been with for many years. In his book, *The New Male Sexuality* (p. 375), the noted sex researcher and therapist, Bernie

Zilbergeld, states, "This may surprise you, but I have been unable to find any evidence to support the notion that for most people, sex in long relationships is less free, less functional, less satisfying than sex among the unattached or sex in affairs." Zilbergeld also reports a study by Louis Harris for *Playboy* that 66% of married men report being very satisfied with their sex lives, compared with 33% of single men. Both men and women in long-term relationships fondly recall when they were dating or recently married, when they were madly in love with one another, and both long to return to that time of intense closeness when they could not be together enough. That time cannot be regained, but the love they had for each other can be deepened even when passion is not easily felt.

I would like to present some of Zilbergeld's suggestions for couples to have a satisfying sex life over many years. For further study, please see his excellent, thoughtful, and very readable book on the subject. The recommendations are:

Prioritizing: Commit to making sex a good part of your life. Be willing to do what it takes to make time for it, and make it fun and satisfying. Stop taking it for granted. This may mean putting something aside because you or your partner are feeling horny, or it may make you late for work, or it may mean that you take an *overnighter* or weekend away—just the two of you. Or, better still, a week's vacation, where you are not bothered by computers, telephones, kids or relatives. Leave the cell phone and the laptop at home.

We are addicted to and even somewhat terrorized by the technical gadgets with which we surround ourselves. I have often recommended that couples have an affair—*with each other*. And this brings up timing—making time for sex. Many married couples act as if all good sex must be spontaneous. Think of an affair. Lovers have to make plans, often elaborate plans, to be together next Wednesday at 3 p.m. Do that with your wife or husband. At least plan, on Tuesday or Wednesday, to have a rendezvous on Friday evening. This does not exclude spontaneous sex, but adds to it.

Relating: If you have read and discussed the previous chapters, you know that working on your relationship is essential to having a good marriage, and it is essential for good sex. We've heard ex-wives and ex-husbands lament, "The only good thing about the marriage was the sex." But they are really thinking of the times when the marriage was good, and so the sex was good, too. All marriages will have bad times as well, but good, long-term marriages last because the couple learned how to reconnect after the bad times. One—or better, both—have learned to quickly reach out to one another. Over the years, I have worked with only one couple who used sex in order to reconnect before talking about what was coming between them. Husbands will often suggest sex as a solution, but wives refuse until they feel close and loving again.

Sometimes we need to isolate sex from at least some of the other negative struggles that worry us. It is important, at times, that we allow ourselves to enjoy sex even though there are unresolved issues. An example might be: the husband has lost his job and the wife is convinced that it was his own fault. It does not help either of them, or the marriage, to withhold the comfort and connecting power of sex because of his possible failure and the wife's disappointment. Another example would be that the husband thinks of something that the wife neglected to do, and brings it up just before their planned romantic rendezvous. He will do himself and his wife a favor to isolate their romantic interlude from his resentment about the undone chore.

Touching: Couples have good sex if they also know the value of, and have developed the habit of, hand-holding, hugs, cuddling, and kisses that are deliberate—not just perfunctory and not just before asking for sex. Hundreds of times I have heard wives complain about their husbands coming up behind them, hugging them from behind, and grabbing their breasts while they are cooking or doing dishes. After reporting this, the wife usually says, "If I act like I appreciate his affection, he wants to have sex." So touching without expecting sex is important. With the touching goes romancing: doing special little things—surprises, cards for no reason, little gifts just because you were thinking of him or her, etc. Set things up so that you anticipate doing things together and, of course, one of the things is making love. I really like the expression *making love* rather than *having sex*—the latter sounds too thing-y to me. And I dislike people saying that a one-night stand is making love or being intimate. From my point of view, it is usually neither. I wonder if heterosexual couples would do themselves a favor if they followed the lead of some gay couples who refer to their partners as *my lover?*

EMPHASIZE PLAYING AND FEELING

Playing: Ideally, a couple does not work at sex but *plays* with sex—in a childlike, playful way. Often, couples did play in their courtship days and then, somehow, their playfulness vanished after the marriage ceremony or the first child was born. Or it was playful until they got close to *going all the way*, and then it became serious or somber. One woman told me that she was taught by her parents and her church that sex was sinful and evil until one was married. "And how," she asked, "was I supposed to suddenly push some kind of 'playful' button and enjoy sex?" Fortunately, she had a very good marriage and, with her patient husband, did learn to enjoy sex. Learning to be playful is frequently a challenge. As mentioned before, sex is fun and natural, but sometimes we have to learn it; or, more accurately, re-learn it, because somewhere, down deep inside us, we know.

Along with being playful, we need to allow our feelings to be spontaneously expressed in our sexual encounters—sometimes we feel fun and giggly, and other times powerfully passionate, and everything in between. Sometimes it can be a pleasurable "quickie" and other times last for hours. In *Yearnings*, Irwin Kula mentions that if we don't allow adventure within our relationship, we'll tend to seek it elsewhere. "When our illicit fantasies are banished from our own bedroom, when we play it safe at home, we'll look for danger somewhere else. And so sex with someone new and forbidden becomes so appealing. Or if we don't dare do that, there's always the titillation of *Desperate Housewives* or pornography." He asks, "What if we could stop dualizing and separating our need for commitment and our need for lust? What if what we really yearn for are lusty commitments and commitments to lust? In order for monogamy to work, sometimes monogamy has to be 'dirty.'" In other words, we need to learn to be sexually playful in lots of ways.

TALKING ABOUT SEX

Whatever their personal history, couples need to talk about their sex lives. Zilbergeld calls this "oral sex"—simply opening one's mouth and saying something about sex. I've found that our feelings and thoughts about sex are some of the most difficult areas to discuss. If even one critical remark has been made about one's body or lovemaking performance, it is like an indelible mark—a brand—that is never forgotten, and grows, like an emotional cancer, inside the offended person. It is a stab at the most intimate part of our being.

I recommend talking about what we enjoy or do not enjoy. This should be often, because we typically feel differently at different times; sometimes we might want to be slow and easy, and other times lusty and fast. Several years ago, Anne and I conducted weekend workshops for couples on enhancing their lovemaking lives. On Friday evenings, we showed two films to facilitate discussion. One was called *A Quickie!* It depicted a couple, dressed like spies, approaching a hotel room from opposite directions. They met at the same door, opened it, and immediately (think *fast-forward*) undressed and began having sex—foreplay, oral sex, intercourse on the bed, on the floor, while standing—all within about three minutes. After looking at a watch, they quickly dressed, overcoats and all, opened the door and walked in opposite directions. Then the title appeared: *A Quickie!* On Saturday morning, a woman in her late sixties, who had attended the Friday evening session with her husband, thanked me for showing that film. She said that she and her husband had been married for over forty years and, "That film pretty much showed the way we've made love all these years." She added, "And last night was the first time I ever had an orgasm!" So, we clearly need to talk about this very important, life-giving part of our lives.

A husband in one of the workshops shared that he had married a wonderful woman who had been raised in a very religious home and had attended a church that would have made the Puritans proud. He was more sexually experienced than his wife, but feared suggesting oral sex. He was sure that she would think he was a pervert for even mentioning it. They had been married for about three years and he finally worked up the courage to tell her that he was interested in oral sex. "And you know what she said?" he reported to the group. We all shook our heads and he said, "She said, 'What are you, some kind of pervert?'" His wife, who was sitting next to him, blushed, and laughed with us.

COMMUNICATE BUT NEVER CRITICIZE

When we talk about sex, we need to follow all the rules of communication as outlined in Chapter 3. Avoid criticism or blaming. Words such as, "If only you'd be more playful (or had larger breasts or penis or went slower, etc.)," should never be spoken. Both men and women are already too critical of their own appearance and sexual performance to be criticized by their partners. One sex researcher quipped that there are only two breast sizes—too big and too small, and only one penis size—too small.

Sex therapists encourage partners to share with their lovers what feels good and what does not. The last time I checked, no sex partner is a mind reader. Some people (mistakenly, I believe) think that they know what all men, or all women, want. This is always wrong. So be courteous, patient, open, and understanding. One couple I worked with had been married over 20 years and reported having a "terrible" sex life "forever." While discussing it, the husband revealed, for the first time, that he was completely turned off on their wedding night when his beautiful new bride put on a very skimpy negligee and offered to go down on him. They were virgins when they got married. He was raised in a very puritanically religious home and she was raised by two liberal parents who even left *Playboy* magazines lying around the house. She assumed that he would be pleased with her suggestive attire and approach, but instead he held a grudge against her for over twenty years, and only then told her about it. So it is important to talk and listen with compassion and understanding.

OUR SEX EDUCATION—A BROAD APPROACH

For our partners to understand us, we need to share our reflections on our own sex education experiences, even if we think our partners already know it, because we are older and more mature (hopefully) than when we talked about it years ago. It is interesting that women usually find it easier than men to talk about the intimate details of their sex lives. Countless times I have heard wives discuss how they really enjoyed oral sex, but their husbands did not. While the wives are talking, their husbands look like they would like to crawl in a hole somewhere. It is not wise, on the other hand, to feel compelled to *confess* to one's spouse—to tell him or her everything you've ever done. And it is neither wise nor helpful to demand that a partner tell his or her spouse every detail about what he or she did with previous partners.

Men can easily joke about sex, but rarely talk directly and easily about their sex lives. I believe that women talk more easily about sex because they are biologically forced to integrate their sex lives into their total lives because of menstruation, childbearing, nursing, and other natural ways of being sexual. Men manage to compartmentalize it and, by doing so, often put it in a special (good) or "dirty" (bad) place. In any event, it is off limits in ordinary male conversation, except for "dirty" jokes.

Our sex education is truly very broad. It is not something separate from our lives, but very integral to our growth in relating to other human beings. It includes comments made to us about how to wash our genitals, modesty in dress, the way we talk about our bodies, etc. I don't know how many times I've heard men describe how they were scolded and even condemned for touching their penis or masturbating. The most common *sin* for young Christian men is masturbation. When an adolescent mentions it to me, I tell him that it's natural and if he's worried about it, learn to enjoy it and forget it. He often reports later that he masturbates less but enjoys it more. It would have been good if he did not have to wait for a counselor to tell him this.

A second, and even more devastating, lesson is witnessing violence between parents. One of the most important and negative lessons about sex came from *not* seeing my father touch my mother, except to hit her. I did not realize that his behavior was a lesson in relationships between men and women until many years later. One of the reasons I waited so long to get married was that I believed it was best that I love everyone and be close to no one. Somewhere, deep in my subconscious, was the belief that to be close to a woman was to hurt her.

So, you can imagine my struggle with Masters and Johnson's statement, "Sex is procreative, communicative, natural, and fun." Now, I'd read enough and talked enough about male and female anatomy to know about sex being procreative, but it took longer for me to really understand that it is "communicative, natural, and fun." Far too many people grow up believing that sex is sinful if it is not open to procreation. I believe that much of the unnatural teachings about sex, and the tradition of seeing the body as evil, can be traced to clergy of all faiths. We are told that in order to conquer our sexual urges, we must demonize the enemy—sex (and, too often, women as well). St. Augustine, an early theologian, stated that men were made in the image of God, but women were not!

The concept that the body is evil or sinful and the soul or spirit is good pre-dates Christianity. It is so sad to see sin equated with sexual transgressions such as *impure* thoughts, masturbation, kissing and so forth, while other, more destructive sins, like injustice, violence, war, assault, etc., are often ignored. I'm guessing that when most people say "We are all sinners," they mean that we are all guilty of impure thoughts, desires, and actions—in other words, that we are sexual beings.

All Christian teachings regarding sex are not negative, however. The emphasis on the sacredness of sex—that is, seeing the sexual union as something beautiful and to be celebrated—is wonderful. This, in my mind, is something that should be kept and not be the-baby-thrown-out-with-the-bathwater (of puritanical attitudes). It seems that religious people have a hard time *baptizing* lust as a positive element of the sexual experience of joy and pleasure. Imagine life-giving sex between two people who have managed to totally subdue their passion and lust. Ironically, it would lose its sacramental and sacred meaning—an outward sign signifying deep love. Without lust, where is the deep, life-giving love? Consider the woman who told me that she grew up thinking sex was totally bad and then, when she got married, she was supposed to be spontaneous and joyful! It took her, and many others, years to flip the switch to joyful sex.

When I was still in college, I heard a lecture in which the speaker compared a person to a helicopter: the large prop on the helicopter keeps it in the air and moving; the small prop in back gives it direction. In humans, the large prop is our emotions, giving us power and movement; the small prop is our intelligence, giving us direction. I like the analogy, but at the time, I thought: *I'm not a helicopter; I'm an army tank, because I haven't gotten off the ground.* I had been too successful in subduing all my emotions—my essential, life-giving energy—in order to subdue my sexual feelings and anger.

I have shared with you, at length, my own journey in overcoming my early education and conditioning in my quest for a healthier attitude toward sex, with the hope that you will also reflect on your own early beliefs and spiritual journey. Be patient with your partner, who has gone through similar or worse life experiences. It is interesting to note that growing up in a family where affection is not shown, or shown infrequently and awkwardly, can affect our attitudes toward sex and intimacy.

THE TRAGEDY OF SEXUAL ABUSE

A conservative estimate is that one in four women has been sexually abused or raped before the age of eighteen. Many researchers, in fact, believe that it is one in three. In any event, it is horribly high, and it is one of the most traumatic crimes that can be committed. What is most terrible is that it devastates the emotional and relational lives of victims. It is of the greatest importance for the husband of a woman who has been violated to be very understanding, patient, and gentle. Of course, these virtues are always important, but even more so in the case of abuse victims. Sometimes even the victim herself will not remember the abuse until she is an adult and has entered into an intimate, sexually expressive relationship. The woman will often find herself reacting to a touch or a verbal expression that triggers a great deal of hurt, fear or anger. This will not only surprise her, but also her partner, who can't figure out what he did wrong. Again, open and caring dialogue is important.

Mental health personnel are finally realizing that childhood sexual abuse is very traumatic and often diagnosed as PTSD—post-traumatic stress disorder. So, it is very important to treat it seriously and, like the woman from the rigid religious background, it can be overcome. It may be important for the couple to seek counseling and for the woman to do some therapy work only for herself. In exploring this, keep in mind that the victim, of any age, is innocent. The guilty party is the perpetrator. She needs to remind herself constantly of this—and her partner needs to deeply understand this and never, ever talk in a way that might imply that she is somehow at fault or bad. Many men have also been sexually abused as children, and they also need tenderness, patience, and understanding.

DIFFERENT ATTITUDES OF MEN AND WOMEN

It is interesting to note the different attitudes men and women have toward sex—different from one another and from other persons of the same gender. Women often expect that the men they are dating, in love with, or married to know all about sex—how to do it, what will please them, etc. This could not be further from the truth. For example, many men and women do not know that an ejaculation and an orgasm are two different things, involving two different nervous systems. Sex researchers usually state that an ejaculation involves a kind of minor

orgasmic response, but not
a total orgasm. So it can
be said that men probably
do not have full orgasms
any more frequently than
women. Get in the mood
by taking your time and
making love when things
are cool—as well as when
they are hot—between you
and your partner, and notice
the pleasurable difference.

Too often, men learn
about sex from pornography.
One of the biggest problems
with pornography is that it
is, for the most part, terrible
sex education. There was a
very humorous review by Al
Martinez in the *L.A. Times* on a book called *Porn for Women*. It was not,
as Martinez said, "An honest-to-God dirty book by the Cambridge
Women Pornography Cooperative, but, 'Prepare to enter our fantasy
world, girls (or guys who want to learn something); a world where
clothes get folded just so, dinners await us at home, and flatulence is
just not that funny.'" It had *erotic* pictures of women enjoying "shirtless,
hunky men bringing them flowers for no reason, leaning in to pay
attention to what they're saying, vacuuming the house and cooking
gourmet dinners." I've done all of these things, except cooking, which I
hate, although I had four brothers who were pretty good at cooking but
lousy at the other things. I do the dishes most of the time, though—
erotic? Hmmm? Anyway, you get the picture. I have yet to find a
woman who enjoys seeing the usual porn film's five-minute scene of

a piston-like penis going in and out of a vagina—usually without a complete torso or head (sometimes with a woman's face acting like she is enjoying it). But please, ladies, patiently re-educate your partner, as his education in this area is usually quite inadequate.

As with all things, patience and understanding are needed, not blame and condemnation—for both sides of the gender-gap.

DISCUSSION TOPICS

- *Share with one another your own sex education journey—education in the broad sense, and not the hour or two about human "plumbing" you received in the sixth grade.*

- *How did your parents show affection toward one another? How did your siblings and friends talk about sex when you were growing up?*

- *Share one or two experiences you have had with your partner that were really wonderful.*

- *What would you like your partner to know about your sexual likes and dislikes?*

- *What time of day do you most enjoy having sex? What is the best setting for you?*

- *How do you like your partner to let you know he or she wishes to make love? Does "Ya wanna get it on, baby?" cut it for you? (If you didn't at least chuckle, you need more humor in your life.)*

- *Plan a rendezvous at home, and one away from home. Include all the details!*

Chapter 6

THEY LIVED HAPPILY EVER AFTER ... BECAUSE THEY WERE OPEN, FLEXIBLE, NON-CONTROLLING, UNPOSSESSIVE, ADVENTURESOME, CREATIVE, AND LOVING

As I was contemplating what I wanted to put in this last chapter— "and they lived happily ever after"—I realized that a happily married couple had all the characteristics of a truly mature person. Abraham Maslow, a psychologist who studied healthy people, stated that after people have their basic needs met, as well as their "being" needs— beauty (art, music, etc.), creativity, spiritual growth, and all the things that are most human—then they are *self-actualized*. I prefer to think that, while we are working to fulfill our basic needs, we are, or should be, developing our "being" needs and becoming a self-actualized person. In other words, ideally, we are continually growing in various ways during our entire lives. So, I would like to take a look at what I consider the characteristics of a self-actualizing marriage, or intimate partnership:

BEING OPEN

As I said before, we need to be open—open to ourselves and to one another. Open to ourselves means accepting our strengths as well as our weaknesses. As mentioned previously, we often grow to adulthood hating a large part of ourselves, and to grow, we need to acknowledge that part of ourselves; otherwise we stay in a constant war with ourselves. If we deny that we have negative or dark parts of ourselves, then *voilà*—we have already discovered a big part of our devilish side: our denial!

The people who think they have no faults and never do anything wrong are very difficult to live with. Characteristically, they would rather be right (at least in their minds) than be happy. They are rigid and expect everyone around them to be rigid as well (to keep all their "rules"). They have absolute opinions about how *good* people, both young and old, should act in all situations. They presume to be very moral and upright citizens, but are steeped in prejudice. Perhaps worst of all, they are not open to change. If one is *perfect* in all thoughts, words, and actions, what need is there to change?

If you believe that this is, at least in part, your dark side, I encourage you to be open to at least two people whom you trust and whom you know love you, and ask them what they think about this idea of openness and your own possible dark side. To change is a painful journey, but worth the effort, for it will open a whole new world for you. Please do not be too quick to declare that person is not you. I believe we all have this tendency.

Acknowledging our anger, destructive desires and actions, is difficult but important. Having these tendencies does not make you a bad person, but it does make you a person in need of change—like everyone else—and it probably makes you difficult to live with. I like the 12-Step Program of Alcoholics Anonymous, and

its insistence on being open to others and to take one day at a time as we work to overcome our weaknesses and addictions. This process can apply to all of our shortcomings. An example would be: Today I am not going to express my anger in the destructive ways I habitually do—especially toward the ones I love, my spouse and children.

Being open to one another takes work, too. Remember the last time someone demanded that you change some habit or way you do something? If you are like me, and most people I've known, you got defensive and angry—even if you didn't show it. So it is with partners. If we wish to help someone (including ourselves) change, first we must accept them (ourselves) as they (we) are. Remember the rosebud blossoming into a full rose model of change? Take a rosebud—or any other flower bud—and try to make it open. You will end up with a pile of petals on the floor. Just as you cannot *make* a flower open, you cannot make another person open. You need to coax and invite him or her to open—nurture that person to open up by providing a safe place. Yelling at them to change or get the hell out doesn't create a very safe place. The other person may go through the actions that they think you desire, but it is not real change. A good parent, as well as a good partner, is like a gardener, not a carpenter. A gardener nurtures the plant and helps it grow; the carpenter pounds it into place.

BEING FLEXIBLE

Perhaps I should have put *being flexible* before *being open*, because flexibility is absolutely necessary to openness. Similarly, openness is necessary for flexibility. The closed person is the one mentioned before who knows all the answers and never does anything wrong or makes any mistakes (as he or she sees it). Let go of your absolute ideas and absolute ways of doing things, and you'll be surprised how much more enjoyable your life will become. People, especially your spouse, will delight in your company!

BEING NON-POSSESSIVE AND NON-CONTROLLING

Over the years, I have been amazed to discover that many couples lived together quite happily for two or more years prior to getting married. Then, almost immediately after going through the wedding ceremony, things changed. They became possessive and controlling in ways they never were before. What happened?

I believe what happened is that each of them held beliefs, often unconsciously, about what it means to be married and to be a husband or wife, and these beliefs blossomed forth after the wedding. Before they were married, they often felt they were free to be with their partners, or to leave their partners without hurting them—at least, not too much. Of course, there are many exceptions among unmarried couples, even teens in high school, who become possessive and controlling partners.

Being free and feeling free are challenging but vital in an intimate relationship. At first, we don't *want* to be free—we want to remain in each other's arms for all of eternity (as the songs say). Of course, that changes. Our tendency, and the concept of marriage we have inherited, is to feel possessive toward our partners. For example, when introducing our partners, we say, "I'd like you to meet my wife/husband." Unfortunately, the emphasis is too often on the possessive pronoun—*my*. We don't really *own* our partners, but there were times in history, and there still are some places on our planet, when the husband literally owns his wife—and she was (is) treated like a slave. "Thou shalt not covet thy neighbor's wife," is followed by, "Thou shalt not covet thy neighbor's goods." I guess it is okay to covet thy neighbor's husband. (A chuckle, please.)

With possessiveness comes control—if I *own* you, then I must control you. This might mean that I (the husband or wife) see this as my duty and responsibility. I need to know where you are at all times and whom you are with and what you are doing, or I am not being a good spouse. I have actually heard spouses say, "I trust him or her because I know exactly where he or she is, and what he or she is doing every minute of the day." That, for me, is not trust, but possessiveness and control.

BEING FREE IN RELATIONSHIPS AND MARRIAGE

Ideally, I should feel freer in marriage than in single life. I am free from constantly seeking companionship as I go places and do things. I have a partner in having and raising children. I need not take all the responsibility to raise the children, keep up the house, pay the bills, and so on. I am free to extend my family by being related to my partner's family (even though, at times, this can be a liability rather than an asset). I extend my circle of friends and acquaintances and thus the number of possible activities I engage in. And, as mentioned in the previous chapter, I have the freedom to develop a wonderful sex life with my partner.

On our honeymoon, Anne and I stayed in a cabin on a lake in the Rocky Mountains. The first day we were there—a beautiful day in late May—we rented a boat and motored around the lake, and then docked the boat near a beautiful forest. Anne and I began hiking through the woods. I discovered that I had this severe pain in my shoulders and neck. We had spent several wonderful weekends together before, and I had never felt this kind of pain during those times. As we were walking and holding hands, I reflected on the source of the pain, and began thinking about being married. My internal voice went something like this: "You are now responsible for another person. You are committed for life, and must care for another person forever." I had the good sense to share these thoughts with Anne and, in her usual insightful way, she said, "I've got an idea. Let's just be married for today, and tomorrow we'll say, 'Let's get married today'—if we want to, that is, so we won't feel trapped or burdened." It was the right thing to say. My pain entirely lifted, and then we really began our honeymoon. For years, every morning we'd ask each other if we wanted to get married today. That was forty years ago, and we rarely say it now—I think we are glad to be stuck with each other.

Another way to be free in marriage is to do things apart as well as together. Women often enjoy a night out with their friends, every couple of weeks or once a month. And guys typically play golf, go to ballgames, or bowl, etc., with their friends. This is healthy. It is good that we have a life apart as well as together, because one person cannot take care of all our emotional and recreational needs. I notice that women often have more friends than their husbands. Husbands may have golfing buddies or friends for other activities, but rarely have really intimate, confidential friends. Guys, if this is you, I encourage you to change this. Of course, there are no "friends of Don" out there. I must go make some friends and invite them out for coffee or lunch...

Another important thing is not to give your partner the third degree when you've been apart. "How was your trip (group, class, outing, etc.)?" is appropriate. But "Where did you go? What did you do? Who were you with? What time did you go to bed?" is not. An open-ended question, which leaves the other person free to share what he or she wishes, is best. It is also important for the one who went out not to just say, "Oh, fine," and refuse to elaborate. A little sharing shows you care and increases your intimacy. After all, we are partners in life.

There are times, of course, when you must be in control, and those times involve your own physical, emotional, and mental health and the health of our children or other family members. These include: When your spouse is hurtful to you or others through his or her drinking, out-of-control anger and brutality, sexual abuse (including spousal rape), compulsive gambling or overspending, and any kind of activity that harms you, your children or other family members. At those times, it is important to take control. You must insist that your partner seeks help—therapy, couples counseling, Alcoholics Anonymous, or any other helpful program. Often, men will not go to therapy by themselves, but will go with their wives. I have had a great deal of success suggesting that wives ask their husbands to go to counseling "for my sake." The husband agrees to go because he really does care, but is unaware how his actions are affecting his spouse or the rest of the family. More women than men are in therapy, and that is not because they need it more, but because they are more aware and willing to admit they need help.

CHILDREN

It is difficult for children to believe that they are really loved if parents rarely spend time with them. Of course, children won't believe it at all if the majority of what they hear from parents are harsh words and criticism. I was ordered out of my own siblings' houses more than once for objecting to my sisters or brothers calling their children "little shits," "snotty brats," "little turds," or hitting them. All of my nieces and nephews are grown now and often comment that they did not feel loved by their parents. Sadly, some of them have repeated the same disastrous cruelty. I've never met a parent who said he or she didn't love his or her children, but I have met many who did not show it very well.

Back in Chapter 2, I mentioned the stages for changing habits. If you find yourself repeating your parents' mistakes, take the time and energy to change your habits. It is worth it for yourself and for your children.

One thing I have often recommended to parents, especially fathers who usually spend less time with their children, is to take a day of the week and do something special with one child. Something like this: Tuesday evening is Special Night with Dad, and they go to the child's favorite place to eat, and go for a walk or play miniature golf, or something else the child enjoys. I recommended this to one father several years ago when his four children were quite young. The oldest two are now in high school, and he still does it, and the children still look forward to it. The only negative (if it's a negative at all) is that the kids want to do it every week instead of every four weeks! Of course, he has a great relationship with his kids. Remember, "Two's company; three's a crowd."

SPECIAL TIMES FOR ONLY THE TWO OF YOU

I stated at the beginning of this chapter that couples live happily ever after because they are adventurous and creative. This applies especially to spending time together, both with the kids and without the kids.

Learn something new together—art classes, golf, tennis, dancing, hiking, whatever you like. Be creative and adventuresome. One couple I worked with in marriage counseling owned a small cabin in the mountains of Southern California. They had a great time whenever they spent a weekend in the mountains. They were happier there than at home—especially during the weekends when they left the kids at home. One time, they visited the local pastor of a small mountain church and asked him about what it was like to live in the mountains, because they were considering moving. The pastor wisely said, "If you are enjoying life now where you live, you will enjoy life up here. If you do not now enjoy life, then you will bring all of your full-time problems with you." I can happily report they began to put more energy into enjoying their full-time life. I have received a nice Christmas card from them each year for over 25 years.

Don't be the old poop played by Henry Fonda in the film, *On Golden Pond,* or like the man on the cruise ship in this story: A rather social and likable fellow took a walk around the ship each morning. The first day, he saw a man looking kind of sad sitting on a deck chair. The walker asked, "How would you like to play some shuffleboard?"

The sad man replied, "Nope. I tried that once, and didn't care for it."

The amiable fellow saw the sad man on the same deck chair the next day and asked, "How about a game of deck tennis? They have a nice court on board."

The old grump said, "Nope. I tried that once, and I didn't care for it."

The third day, there was the sad man, sitting on the same chair and looking exactly the same. "How about taking a swim in the ship's pool?" said the sociable man. "It's a beautiful pool."

The sad man replied, "Nope. I tried that once with my son, and I didn't like it."

The stroller said, "Oh, you have a son! Only one, I presume."

I've seen divorced men and women, after being "old poops" during their first marriage, begin to branch out after the divorce. I invariably wonder why they didn't get off their duffs in the first place. I hope that, the second time around, they don't go back to their old ways.

If you begin to see yourselves becoming an old poop, I suggest you look at your love life from different angles. How are your feelings of passion, intimacy, and commitment? In *Love and Communication in Intimate Relationships,* Robert Steinberg divides love into three components: passion, intimacy, and commitment. **Passion** is "the motivational component that fuels romantic feelings, physical attraction, and desire for sexual interaction." It is the deep desire to be united with your loved one. In a sense, passion is an addiction.

Intimacy is "the emotional component of love that encompasses the sense of being bonded with another person, including feelings of warmth and emotional closeness." **Commitment** refers to the decision to love another and to maintain a relationship over time despite difficulties—or, as the traditional marriage ceremony states, "in joy or in sorrow, for richer or for poorer, in sickness and health, 'til death do us part." Passion is the element that often seems to be missing, and was addressed in the previous chapter. Steinberg states that it is normal for passion to peak early in a relationship and then decline, whereas intimacy and commitment continue to build gradually over the years. I believe that this is true for the most part, but a couple can also have a passionate desire to keep their relationship open and fresh.

Keep the Creative Juices Flowing

Both as individuals and as a couple, it is important to keep the creative spirit in our lives—physically, emotionally, intellectually, and spiritually. Everyone has some talent, and it is usually fun to get into the process of learning a new skill or art form. It could be woodworking, painting, gardening, dancing, interior decorating, collecting your favorite things, traveling, the theater (as a playgoer, as an actor, or behind the scenes), sports, community service clubs, writing ; the list is endless. Fortunately, we are living in a time and in a country where we can reinvent ourselves many times. In 1900, the average life expectancy for adults was around 45 years. Now we can expect to live to 80 or longer—that's plenty of time to learn another language, travel overseas, or learn belly dancing!

Encourage each other to get involved in the family, the community, and the world through art, music, volunteering, sports, mentoring, or an array of activities limited only by your imagination. Be creative and adventuresome—you will live happily ever after! Don't discourage your partner from enjoying a particular activity just because you don't share his or her enthusiasm. It can be hurtful to the marriage if you criticize your partner's efforts to be creative and to expand their interests. Give them your full support.

Don't Sweat the Small Stuff

A friend of ours says that there are three kinds of problems. They are:

1. **Everyday problems:** spilling juice on the new carpet; overdrawing the checking account; having a non-injury-causing car accident; catching a cold; falling down and scratching a knee or tearing a pant leg. This

is any problem that is an inconvenience, but where no one was hurt (or hurt seriously).

2. **Serious problems, but from which you can recover:** a broken leg; a surgery that takes several days or weeks to heal; the roof blowing off the house; bankruptcy; losing a job. All are serious and take courage, hard work, and patience to recover from, but you *can* recover—and even become stronger.

3. **Very serious problems from which you cannot recover:** a terminal illness that cannot be cured; a death in the family; serious abuse that sends a family member to prison; suicide. You get the idea.

The reason I mention this way of seeing problems is to put things in perspective. Many people treat everyday problems as if they were serious or very serious problems—everything, to them, is a catastrophe. They sweat the small stuff.

BEING LOVING

We live happily because we live lovingly. We give and receive lots of hugs and compliments; we nurture others and are nurtured in return. We need to give "strokes" (*attaboys*, encouragement and praise) to one another and to everyone in our lives. It is usually easier to give compliments than to receive them. When someone gives us a compliment, we often discount it: "I really like your shirt."

"Oh, it's just something I picked up at a discount store."

Learn to receive strokes. A simple *thank you* is fine. Learn to ask for strokes, as well (although this can be difficult): "How do you like the tomatoes? They are fresh from our garden!" (If you don't like garden-fresh tomatoes, you're a nut.)

Feel free to *recycle* strokes—right now, take a moment to remember what it felt like when your child ran up to you, gave you a big hug and said, "I love you, Mommy (or Daddy)!"

Laugh at Yourself

I know that when a client or a couple begin to laugh at themselves, they are beginning to overcome the depression, anxiety, or whatever it was that brought them into counseling. It is truly difficult to be sad and laugh at ourselves at the same time. Just think of the goofy things we do. And if you never do goofy things, well, start doing them. Our lives are much happier when we stop taking ourselves seriously.

Along with this, we need to learn to play. Now, in the 21st century, we have the time to play.

Maybe we always did, but again, our country's puritanical background made it seem almost sinful to play. An anthropologist, writing about a tribe in the Amazon basin of Brazil, discovered that the people used the same word for work and play. She described a trip through the jungle where she and her entourage, both American and native, had to forage around a waterfall. The Americans were swearing and complaining as they carried the canoes and gear around the falls, while the natives sang and laughed and made a game of it. I'm sure you can think of many ordinary household and yard chores that can be made into games, or at least be made lighter. Even if you are a terrible singer, sing! It is impossible to be depressed and sing at the same time. And if you don't sing very well, laugh as others comment on your performance.

I hope that these ideas have been helpful to you as a couple, or helpful to even one partner. When you share your thoughts, please be respectful and non-blaming as you speak. And, of course, as you listen!

If, after great and good faith work on both your parts, you decide that the most creative and life-giving thing for you both is to separate, please do not consider your life together and the effort you've put in as wasted. Hopefully, you have learned a great deal about yourself and about life, and because of your time together, you both are healthier and more mature people. I believe that divorce is a last resort, to be considered when all else fails, especially if you have children, although children benefit more from the attention of two happy parents living apart than from two parents who live together unhappily and antagonistically.

DISCUSSION POINTS

- *Share thoughts on two or three couples who you think are creative, playful, and adventuresome. Include people from films or stories.*

- *What are some ways that you allow yourself to be closed and inflexible? Share your thoughts with your spouse—and graciously accept any suggestions he or she may have.*

- *How are you sometimes possessive and/or controlling?*

- *What are some things you often thought of doing when you were young that you have not done and still wish to do?*

- *How would you like to hear your partner say, "I love you!" How often?*

- *What are some dreams you have about growing old together? What will your "empty nest" be like?*

- *Now what are you going to do?*

I hope that you are feeling more hopeful about your own growth and future as a couple, and that you are now listening to each other and problem solving together, and being open and flexible. I hope that love is being expressed and shared in an easy and relaxed way that is joyful for everyone. I hope that you are having so much fun that it is *sinful* as you walk into the sunset and *live happily ever after!*

SUGGESTIONS FOR FUTURE READING

On Becoming a Person, Carl Rogers

Peoplemaking, Virginia Satir

Seven Principles for Making Marriage Work, John Gottman

The Intimate Enemy, George Bach and Peter Wyden

Getting the Love You Want, Harville Hendrix

The Art of Loving, Erich Fromm

Do I Have to Give up Me to Be Loved by You? Jordan and Margaret Paul

The Velveteen Rabbit, Margery Williams

ACKNOWLEDGEMENTS

In this book, I have used ideas from many people–special mentors such as Carl Rogers, Virginia Satir, Erving Polster, and many others– and, when appropriate, I have noted sources. To make this guide more informal and easy to read, I deliberately did not use footnotes or formal page references, and I hope that this does not offend anyone. I wish to give special thanks to Niehl Zulueta for his wonderful illustrations, and to Teri Rider for the beautiful cover art. I am also very grateful to many others who have given excellent suggestions and editing help, especially Kim Forgette, Emily Corner, Natalia Park, and Lori Naylor. I am especially grateful for the patience, understanding, and loving heart of my wonderful wife of 45+ years, Anne.

Don Hanley

ABOUT THE AUTHOR

Don Hanley is the ninth of ten children and a "child of the depression," born in 1933 in Nebraska.

His father died when Don was fourteen and he took on the responsibility of taking care of his mother and youngest sister. He yearned to become a priest and after years of working in a lumber yard and as a carpenter, he entered the seminary at age twenty-three. He is the only one in his family to attend college and earned a B.A. in Philosophy, STB in Theology, M.A. in Education, and a Ph.D. in Human Behavior. He was ordained a Catholic priest in 1964 and after six years, left the priesthood to marry. He and his wife have two grown daughters. Don is a licensed Marriage and Family Therapist who has taught graduate courses in psychology and continues to supervise counseling Interns at a California college.

He is now learning how to enjoy being an old man.

His other writings include: *Love By Its First Name*, a novel, and non-fiction: *How To Live With Yourself And Enjoy it.*

www.ingramcontent.com/pod-product-compliance
Lightning Source LLC
Chambersburg PA
CBHW032101020426
42335CB00011B/445